Christmas Memories

Stories of Newfoundland and Labrador

Lisa J. Ivany
&
Robert J. Hunt

CREATIVE PUBLISHERS

St. John's, Newfoundland
2004

©2004 Lisa Ivany & Robert Hunt

The Canada Council | Le Conseil des Arts
for the Arts | du Canada

We acknowledge the support of The Canada Council for the Arts for our publishing program.

We acknowledge the financial support of the Government of Canada through the Book Publishing Industry Development Program (BPIDP) for our publishing program.

Cover Art & Design: Joanne Snook-Hann
∞ Printed on acid-free paper

Published by
CREATIVE PUBLISHERS
an imprint of CREATIVE BOOK PUBLISHING
a Transcontinental Inc. associated company
P.O. Box 8660, St. John's, Newfoundland A1B 3T7

First Printing October 2004

Typeset in 11.5 point Book Antiqua

Printed in Canada by:
Transcontinental Inc.

National Library of Canada Cataloguing in Publication

Ivany, Lisa J., 1965-
Christmas memories : stories of Newfoundland and Labrador / Lisa J. Ivany & Robert J. Hunt.

ISBN 1-894294-81-5

1. Christmas--Newfoundland and Labrador. 2. Christmas--Literary collections. I. Hunt, Robert J., 1949- II. Title.

GT4987.15.I83 2004   394.2663'09718
C2004-905942-4

TABLE OF CONTENTS

Dedications vi
Acknowledgements...vii
Work of Fiction vii

Roses for Rose 1
Sonata for Two...5
Tis the Season...11
Becky's Wish 18
Poetry – Candy Cane Kisses 21
Dustin's Christmas Spirit 22
Only One Heartbeat 29
Winking Light...35
Christmas Trivia 39
Note From Santa 40
Love is Blind...45
Billy's Answer (To Becky's Wish).............................54
An Elf in Hiding 59
Poetry – My Christmas Angel 67
A Mission of Love 68
Letting Go 75
The Cross 81
Christmas Trivia 85
Lucky's Surprise 86
The Lottery 95
Maggie's Bread...101
In the Heat of the Moment..106
Poetry – Christmas Eve Journey 113
A Helping Hand 114
Christmas Heartbeat 123
A Winning Spirit...126
Christmas Trivia 135

One Rainy Night..136
Hazard Mountain 144
Poetry – If the Innkeeper Only Knew 155
Christmas Trivia 156
Festive Flavours..157

Appetizers

Nacho Dip...158
Hot Swiss Dip 158
Pine-Nutty Cheese Ball.......................................159
Saucy Wieners...159

Brunch

Japanese Chicken Salad 160
Broccoli Salad 160
Layered Salad..161
Baked Holiday Omelet 161
French Onion Soup..162
Cheesy Chowder..163
Barbecue Chicken Wraps 163
Turkey Chunkers...164

Vegetable Dishes

Turnip Casserole..165
Vegetable Cheese Loaf..165
Festive Vegetables 166
Hash Brown Casserole...167

Main Courses

Bubbly Fish Bake 168
Glazed Salmon 168
Boxing Day Casserole 169

Pineapple Pork Casserole 170
Cranberry Pork Chops 170
Crowned Pork and Dressing 171
Cheesy Beef and Mac 172
Creamy Beef and Broccoli 172
Cheddar Beef Pie 173
Steak and Peppers 174
Stuffed Roll 175
Spaghetti Bake 175
Pizza Casserole 176
Chicken Lasagna 177

Desserts

Chewy Snowballs 178
Five Star Squares 179
Maggie's Chocolate Marshmallow Roll 179
Toffee Squares 180
Bounty Bars 180
Pecan Tarts 181
Chocolate Drops 182
Toffee Bar Dessert 182
Seaweed Pie 183
Neapolitan Ice Cream Cake 183
Pistachio Trifle 184
Chocolate Temptation 185
Peachy Cool Dessert 185

Gift Basket Ideas 187
Inexpensive Stocking Stuffers 189
Christmas Card Register 190

DEDICATION 1

To my very good friend, Lisa, whose inspiration made this book possible and who, I think deep down, because of her kind heart and nature, believes that there still is a Santa Claus.

To my wife, Sharon, and children, Stephen and Heather, who agreed that this book was a wonderful idea and for the inspiration they gave me to write it. Now that it's finally complete, thanks for your patience while I spent many hours in front of the computer.

- Robert J. Hunt

DEDICATION 2

To my co-author, who started out as an acquaintance, became my mentor, and now is a very dear friend. Bob, it's been a pleasure working with you and I've enjoyed your talent, guidance, and especially your wonderful wit.

To my mother, who has been a tremendous support from start to finish. Thanks for tolerating my numerous periods of seclusion while working on this book and for preparing all the wonderful meals when I've been too busy to cook. My confidence as a writer is partly attributed to all the encouragement and understanding you have given me over the years and I love you for it.

Finally, in memory of my father, who always told me to follow whatever dreams would make me happy. It's taken me a while to get here, but dad, I've been listening. Wherever you are, I know you're watching with pride from above and because of you, heaven's stars now shine brighter.

- Lisa J. Ivany

ACKNOWLEDGEMENTS

A special thanks goes to Bob Gill for his assistance and support. A sincere note of gratitude is extended to Bev Noseworthy, who introduced the two authors. Without that introduction, this book would surely not have been written. Finally, thanks to Frank Galgay, Cal Smith, Janice Brien, Marilyn Anthony, Carol Noseworthy, and Kelly Jamieson for reading our manuscript in its infancy stage. Your feedback and suggestions have helped prepare us on our road to publication.

WORK OF FICTION

The stories in this book are works of fiction. Any similarity to actual incidents, and any resemblance to persons living or dead is purely coincidental. However, the stories *Maggie's Bread*, *Winking Light* and *Christmas Heartbeat* are based on fact.

ROSES FOR ROSE
(By Lisa J. Ivany)

Being the owner of Bennett's Flower Shop in Springdale, Simon had seen hundreds of customers pass through his door over the years. However, there was a special one he always remembered.

The day before Christmas, exactly 15 years ago today, Simon was arranging flowers in the back room when he heard the bell signalling the arrival of a customer. Already behind schedule, he muttered under his breath at the intrusion as he went to the front counter. At first he didn't see anyone, until a tiny movement of blonde curls caught his attention, just barely reaching the counter top. He leaned over to see a little girl, who looked to be no more than seven years of age.

His demeanor was one of vexation as he stared down at the child. He was really behind with his orders and impatiently asked, "What can I do for you?"

"I'd like to buy a red rose for my mommy," she replied.

"Well little girl, how much money do you have?"

"I have four dollars sir," she said as she fished around in her pocket to extract the cash. A look of bewilderment crossed her face as she failed to retrieve the coins. "Oh no! There's a hole in my pocket and my money's gone!"

In mounting frustration, Simon said, "Even if you hadn't lost your money, it wouldn't be enough. The roses are five dollars each. Now, I have a lot of work to do. Good day." With that, he spun around and returned to the work room.

When he started back at his task of flower arranging, he realized how abrupt he was with the little girl and felt ashamed of his actions. This time of year has always found him in a disgruntled frame of mind with the busy rush of holiday orders and agitated customers. Still, he should not have been so nasty to that sweet little child.

Then he heard a voice whisper to him from the doorway, "Mister, it's really important that I get a rose for my mom. Would I be able to work for the rose, perhaps help you out in your shop?" she pleaded.

Overcome by the pitiful tone of her voice, he relented, "If you're going to help me out, you can start by telling me your name."

"It's Molly Delaney."

"Okay Molly, why don't you sit here at the table and sort these flowers in bundles by colour and tell me why it's so important that you get your mom a rose."

Gratefully, Molly climbed up onto the stool to begin her chore. She started, "I only get to visit my mom once a year, on Christmas Eve. You see, me and my daddy live far away and we can only afford the plane ticket once a year to see her. Maybe that's a good thing because he cries every time we visit, and he looks so sad. We both tell her how much we love her and miss her. She doesn't answer, but daddy says she loves us too." Molly, having finished with her story, said, "My mommy loves roses, especially the red ones. It's probably because her name is Rose too."

Simon wondered why she was living apart from

her mother. He assumed her parents were divorced and asked, "Why don't you live with your mommy?"

"I can't live with her because she's at the cemetery. My dad told me she's happy there because she's an angel and there are lots of other angels in the field with her so she's not lonely."

With a saddened heart, Simon questioned, "What happened to your mommy?"

Molly continued, "She was hit by a car when she was walking home from work on Christmas Eve a long time ago. That's why we pick this day to visit her. I was only two years old at the time so I don't remember much, but I keep a picture of her by my bed so I can look at her before I go to sleep each night. Not long after that, my dad got a new job so we had to move away and we can't visit mommy as much as we want to."

Simon realized he should be grateful for the blessings he had in his life. At 40 years of age, he had both parents still living while this little girl was cheated out of a mother's love at such an early age. He decided that he would stop feeling sorry for himself and never take his family for granted again. He saw how well she had organized the flowers and said, "Okay sweetie, I think you've more than earned your rose. In fact, you've done enough work for twelve roses."

He went to the cooler and brought out his best Christmas arrangement endowed with one dozen beautiful red roses.

"Wow!" Molly exclaimed. "Are they really for my mom?"

Through heavy-misted eyes, he responded, "Yes indeed. Only the best roses for Rose."

They went to the front of the store just as a man entered. He looked relieved as he said, "Molly, I've been looking for you everywhere."

"I'm sorry I wandered off daddy, but I wanted to

get a rose for mom." She held out the flowers for him to view.

"Honey, that's a lot more than one rose. I'm sure you don't have the money to pay for such a large bouquet," her father mentioned.

Simon explained, "Sir, your daughter has been a tremendous help to me this afternoon and worked hard for these flowers. Please accept them with my gratitude."

"Thank you for your kindness. I'm sure my wife will love them."

As Molly headed out the door with her father, she turned around and said, "Merry Christmas, Simon."

He responded, "Merry Christmas Molly. Come back and see me next year." He returned to his work area once more to create another arrangement for his mother to replace the one on its way to a field of angels.

That was so many years ago, but a Christmas Eve Simon will never forget. His business has flourished since then, to the point where he hired a young assistant three years ago. It's his
assistant now who brings him out of his reverie, planting a kiss on his cheek as she prepares to leave. Smiling at him with genuine affection, she says, "Merry Christmas, Simon."

He replies, "Merry Christmas, Molly. Don't forget the roses for Rose."

- LJI

SONATA FOR TWO
(By Robert J. Hunt)

Damian's hands flowed over the piano keys as Beethoven's Piano Sonata, *Appassionata*, overtook his mind and soul. He tried to adjust to the lyrics and notes to suit the keys but each time his hands betrayed him. He forced himself to maintain control of the music to be transferred from mind to body to hands, but it was useless. It seemed Beethoven himself was laughing at him from the grave.

Damian Blackwood was a master pianist who had played before royalty, heads of state, and nearly every prominent figure in Canada. He had taught the "unteachable" to play, making them "hear" the music and lyrics with their soul to allow it to flow forth from their minds to their hands and to the piano keyboard. Over the years, he had taken ordinary players and transformed them into magnificent pianists. Praise had been given to him from other gifted piano players who said that he captured the great composers' music such as Bach and Beethoven as if they were the ones playing to the audience.

Still, try as he may, the one score of music that he could not cultivate was Beethoven's Piano Sonata *Apassionata*. For years he had tried concerto but he had never played it to his satisfaction and had barely given the music its due when playing it as the great masterpiece that it was. To make matters worse, arthritis in his hands had made playing quite painful. Everyday this past two years was agony when he played for more than a few minutes. Beethoven's sonata took approximately 15 minutes to play, create, and react to with satisfaction. As he played, he remembered the hundreds of students to whom he had taught the piano to and the few "chosen" who had gone on to fame as teachers of others. Even now he remembered many of his former students who received awards in their field of expertise in music. He received many calls from all over Canada and the United States asking for concert appearances for special galas to honor distinguished pianists and composers whose music he had refined.

He was renowned in Newfoundland as its most gifted pianist of the quarter century and was to receive the Beethoven Conservatory Of Music Award for gifted musicians and induction into the Newfoundland Music Hall Of Fame on December 20th, just a few weeks away. He just wished his son could be there to see it, but he was now living in Winnipeg, Manitoba and had his own music school to run. But he had phoned to congratulate his father and to wish him well on his special night.

As he played, his mind focused on David and how he had some difficulty taking to the piano. But with his guidance and patience he had come to love music and as he said to his father, he adjusted to the music "to be in touch with his soul." David had played with the Newfoundland Symphony Orchestra of which Damian was once conductor and piano teacher for many years. Damian took great care in making David his protege. He never forced music on him but rather let him understand and learn it on his own. To his surprise, after four months, he became a quick learner and at an early age was teaching his skills to other children, all of whom were less fortunate than he. David's mother, Loretta, spent many hours playing the violin and cello to accompany him with his music on piano.

Many thoughts passed through Damian's mind as he tracked through the past years and remembered it all with great fondness. He just wished that David could be there for his induction eremony on the 20th, but he had his school and family to think of and could not make it. Damian concluded his sonata with a final key stroke and looked at his slightly swollen knuckles and closed the piano cover. One day, he thought, I will master Beethoven's *Apassionata* and it will be my final greatest triumph! He slowly walked away from the piano and met Loretta coming in from the garden where they both had spent many nights talking of their life, their son, and music.

He embraced her gently and said., "Come, mother, let us sit on the swing and talk of David and the grandchildren. Let us talk of life and spending time together when I retire next month. Last of all, let us speak of *Apassionata* and why Ludwig von Beethoven tricked me so to make his sonata the hardest score for me to conquer." He said the last part with a wink in his eye to his wife of thirty-two years.

The next few days when Damian awoke, the numbness in his fingers had become unbearable. When he played, it was with great difficulty. He knew it was only a matter of time when he would only be a teacher to his pupils and would have to let one of his students play for the others while he coached him with his music. Some days were better than others, but he knew that the arthritis would one day render his hands powerless for playing his beloved music. The morning of the 20th

arrived quicker than Damian had anticipated. The man of music became nervous of how he would react tonight when they asked him to play a piano score. His mind would be willing, but he wondered if his fingers would allow it. That night, he entered the Arts & Culture Center amid a chorus of applause. He and Loretta stopped many times to address prominent people who came here to pay respects to him.

They sat in reserved seats by the front of the stage. A few moments later the concert to honor him began. For an hour the audience was given an abundant array of sounds as classical music and choirs sang and played to the beautiful tunes of Bach, Beethoven, and Brahm. Damian was raised up to music heaven. It felt as if the notes drifted across the medium to his ears only and he was filled with inner peace. Half-way through the concert, he turned to Loretta and said quietly.

"This is remarkable. I feel as if I am 20 years old again and just starting music school all over. I just wish that David could be here tonight with us to share this wonderful gala."

"Yes, dear," Loretta said, "I guess you could say David is here with us in heart and soul."

She smiled at her husband and with a wave of her hand the music stopped as the last note of "Blue River" had concluded. Damian looked toward the stage as it darkened and all was quiet. A single blue light shone on a spot on the middle of the floor. The announcer walked towards the center of the stage and spoke.

"Ladies and gentleman. We have something very special for you tonight. A young gentleman asked us if he could perform here tonight to honor Mr. Blackwood. So without further fanfare, I would like to present to you Mr. David Blackwood, Damian Blackwood's son."

Damian sat in awe from the darkened auditorium as David stood up from the piano, walked to the edge of the stage, and looked at the audience and his father.

"Yes, it is really me, dad," he smiled and looked at the gathering. "Ladies and gentleman, mom and dad ... for years I have lived in a home with these two wonderful people who taught me how to love, understand people, and of course, play music. Growing up, my father became my hero, not only because of the music he created in me, but the love he showered on everyone he knew with his music. I found a unique gift inside myself and with that in mind, I wish to play a score especially for you dad, something that mom and I are sure that you will like."

David turned and walked back to the piano, sat down and started Beethoven's *Apassionata*. His fingers glided over the keyboard and the audience became spellbound. Tears came to Damian's eyes as he heard the score played as he had never heard it played before. The piano keys vibrated with sound and meaning and the music engulfed Damian and became a part of him. His soul blended with *Apassionata* as if he and the music were one. He was sent into a hypnotic state of euphoria that he had never experienced in his music lifetime. Then as quiet as it started, the music stopped. David walked from the piano to the edge of the audience and took his father's hand. He walked with him to the piano and waved to him to be seated. Not a sound was heard in the center.

Damian sat at the keyboard. He felt as if he were floating. He commanded control of every part of his body and the stiffness left his fingers. He started to play *Apassionata* as he had never played it before. His hands controlled the keys as rhythm and harmony were guided by him and him alone. He was lost in a world of music and euphoria that few musicians ever reach. No pain, no hurt, just an immense drive to play forever. By the time he was three minutes into the piece, the audience was on its feet clapping and shouting their bravo's toward the stage. Damian was lost in the music as he had never been before. His heart felt alive as the music took over his soul. When he came to the conclusion of *Apassionata*, the audience erupted into a chorus of joy such as none had ever witnessed. Damian played the final note in tears and he felt he would never be able to duplicate this "high" again in his lifetime. For many moments the crowd raved on as Damian finished, stood up, walked to his son, and embraced him.

"David, you have given me the gift of life itself tonight. You have made this the happiest Christmas in my life. I love you. Thank you so much, my son."

"You're welcome, dad. I love you and Merry Christmas to you, too."

- RJH

TIS THE SEASON
(By Lisa J. Ivany)

"Quick, dive behind the desk!" exclaims Vera Stone as she catapults into Lori Brenton's office. "He's coming and he's armed with mistletoe!"

"Who are you talking about?"

"Jerry, who do you think?" she retorts in an exasperated tone. She grabs Lori's arm and yanks her to the floor behind the protection of the oak work station. Huddled in confinement, both women breathe a sigh of relief as they hear Jerry's off-key rendition of *A Holly Jolly Christmas* pass by their seemingly empty haven.

Lori whispers, "Don't you think it's a little ridiculous for two professional 24-year-old women to be hiding under a desk, avoiding the office clown?"

Laughing, Vera counters, "Probably, but think of the consequences if we didn't. Right now, we could be wrestling Jerry under the mistletoe while having our tonsils wrapped up in his sticky wet tongue!"

She heads for the door, saying, "I guess it's safe to go back to the ninth floor now. Apparently he's working his way down all the floors, wrecking havoc wherever he goes. By the time he gets back to sorting the mail on the first floor, he should be exhausted," she chuckles. "I'll see you later at the party."

As Vera exits, Lori peeps out through her blinds to ensure Jerry is a safe distance away. She witnesses his progress by the scattering of female employees down the length of the corridor. She watches him in wonderment as he tries to embrace one girl after another for a yuletide kiss, with very little success.

Jerry's reputation precedes him as the joke of the office here at Fuller's Printing in St. John's, New-found-land. He does little to denounce this title and actually seems to relish in the attention. This is evident today in his outlandish outfit of bright yellow suspenders, supporting cranberry-coloured trousers, three inches too short, and a black tee-shirt with white polka dots. Completing this ensemble are two odd-matched socks of green and brown. To capture his image on film would be like viewing an explosion of vomitus crayons.

Not to be outdone by his wardrobe, Jerry's hair has been gelled to plaster consistency with spiked peaks extruding in disarrayed sections, topped with shades of pink, blue, and green. This, combined with purple-rimmed spectacles that even Elton John would be loathe to wear, portrays quite a rarity of the human species indeed.

Finding the coast to be clear, Lori settles back in her role as a graphics designer to finish off her last project before leaving early for Christmas Eve. She is looking forward to this evening's party at Vera's house where she can kick up her heels and let loose after the extensive overtime she has worked during the past two weeks.

After turning off the lights and locking up, Lori strolls out to the fifth floor elevator in a jovial mood, looking forward to her vacation. As she pushes the button, she notices a set of keys on the floor that someone must have dropped. She stoops to pick them up and recognizes a big yellow happy face key ring, always toted by Jerry. With an inward groan, she realizes she must bring them down to Jerry and risk the mistletoe attack.

Arriving at the main lobby, Lori reluctantly steers herself towards the Mail Room, only to find it has already closed for the holidays. Knowing Jerry will need his key to get into his apartment, she finds herself in an unenviable situation. She seems to be the last one to leave the building so there is no one with whom she can turn over the keys. She resigns herself to the fact that she must seek out Jerry. Although she has never been to his place, she knows his address by heart as he has so often reiterated this fact to all the girls in the office, hoping to find someone desperate enough to visit him.

She starts to walk the four blocks, wondering if Jerry will notice the missing keys and back track, thereby shortening the distance she must travel. However, she has no such luck as she reaches his building and proceeds to his apartment down a long dimly-lit hallway. Lori raps on his door, not expecting an answer considering she has his keys. She knocks once more and the door is opened by a tall dark-haired man, tousling his hair dry while beads of water course down his muscular torso to the towel gathered at his trim waist.

"Lori? I'm surprised to see you here," he states incredulously.

"Is that you, Jerry?" she asks dumbfounded. She didn't recognize him at first in his state of undress and seemingly normal appearance. "You dropped your keys and I thought you might need them to get in."

"That's mighty nice of you. I didn't realize I had lost them until I got home and then I asked my landlady to let me in with her master key. Thanks so much for your trouble." He steps aside and asks, "Would you like to come in for a cup of hot chocolate?"

"No thanks. I have a party to get to."

"Can't you stay a few minutes. The water is just about boiled and I promise to be on my best behavior. Don't worry, I'm all out of mistletoe," he laughs.

Not wanting to be rude and feeling a sense of pleading in his voice, she succumbs and replies, "Okay, but I can only stay for a minute."

"Just give me a moment to put some clothes on and I'll be right back," he says while walking down the hall to his bedroom. He calls out, "Make yourself at home."

Lori settles herself on the sofa, wondering if she has made the right decision, but before she can make a hasty retreat, he enters the room. Dressed in designer jeans and a black wool sweater, he's the epitome of a model for men's clothing and the complete opposite of the geek she frequently encounters at work. She feels as though her mouth is hanging to the floor in utter astonishment.

He notices her expression and explains, "The guy you see every day at the office is not the real me. Before you, stands the real Jerry Stansfield and I hope it's not too much of a let down."

"Let down?" she exclaims. "You look so normal! I'm sorry, I didn't mean that the way it came out."

"That's okay. I know I'm a bit of a nerd-ball at work, but there's a good reason for it."

He heads to the kitchen and pours up two steaming cups of Irish Cream-flavored hot chocolate, topped with whipped cream and chocolate sprinkles. He passes one to Lori and offers her a seat at the table.

She says, "Well, don't keep me in suspense. Why are you so different at work and why don't you let everyone there see this side of you?"

"That's the problem; if I portray who I really am at the office, then no one will notice me. I'm actually quite an introvert and someone who most would find quite boring. I worked for a large firm in Toronto for 10 years and up until I started to work at Fuller's two years ago, no one knew I existed. The place I worked previously was another large company and it's really difficult to make friends in a big city when you don't know anyone. After eight years of working with people who didn't know I existed, I decided to leave and try another approach in my next job. That's when I decided to create a new image that would be hard to ignore, even if it's not looked upon favorably. At least I'm being noticed now and no longer feel like the *Invisible Man*."

Lori empathizes with his situation and is filled with an immense urge to reach out to him. She says, "I'm going to a Christmas party at Vera's and I would love it if you would accompany me, provided you go as you are dressed now and not the fake persona from the office."

"I don't know."

"Come on, Jerry. Most of the people attending are from the firm so you'll know them and you will also have a chance to meet some new people," she implores.

He hesitates, "I don't think they want me there or they would have invited me."

"The Jerry from the office wasn't invited, but I'm sure the *real* Jerry would be quite welcomed and this would give you a chance to prove you exist."

Realizing she is not about to take no for an answer, he relents. "Well, when you put it that way, how can I refuse?"

As they enter Vera's home, the party is in full swing with most of the guests already infused with merriment from the consumption of several glasses of eggnog.

Vera greets Lori, saying, "Merry Christmas. Who's your friend?"

"This is my date, Gerald," Lori answers.

Not recognizing this handsome stranger, Vera warmly says, "Nice to meet you, Gerald. Come on in and make yourself at home."

Throughout the evening, Jerry is introduced to several of his colleagues as Gerald and no one associates him with the bizarre man from the Mail Room. When Lori and Jerry prepare to leave, they are besieged by numerous party invitations to be held over the Christmas holidays. Vera pulls Lori to one side and whispers, "I really like your friend. He's so charming and I feel as if I've known him for a long time."

Lori is still giggling at this remark as Jerry walks her to her door. He says, "Thanks for a wonderful evening. I appreciate it more than you can imagine."

The remainder of the Christmas season sees Jerry attending many social events with Lori. This is the first Christmas he has enjoyed for over 10 years and he owes it all to a special lady who has taken the time to get to know him. He's even warmly accepted into the Brenton household when Lori brings him to her folks' place in Marystown for a couple of days during the holidays. By the time New Year's Eve arrives, the ruse is up and everyone knows who Gerald really is and they have a whole new perception of him. Indeed, they now consider him a friend and all agree they like this new version they see.

Lori and Jerry's last party of the year is New Year's Eve in the firm's large banquet room. During a slow dance, as the midnight hour arrives, bells ring to herald in the new year and balloons and confetti fall to the floor. Through the cacophony of noisemakers and the strains of *Auld Lang Syne*, Lori retrieves a piece of mistletoe from her pocket and lifts it above Jerry's head. She raises her voice above the noise to say, "Happy New Year, Jerry. I didn't get my Christmas kiss from you, so how about a New Year's kiss?"

Shyly, he leans forward and softly grazes her lips briefly with his. As he starts to raise his head, Lori laces her fingers behind his neck and tugs softly, until his mouth once again covers her own. Moments later, while still locked in a comfortable embrace, Jerry asks, "So what's your New Year's resolution?"

Without hesitation, Lori responds, "To avoid making judgments about people before getting to know them. How about you?"

Pulling her closer, he replies, "To make sure you don't forget I exist."

- LJI

BECKY'S WISH

(By Robert J. Hunt)

Dear Santa Claus:

My name is Becky, I'm nine years old, and you don't have to check your naughty book because daddy and mommy said that I have been a good girl all year. I'm letting my Aunt Violet help me write to you. I want to write to you early because you are so busy and to see if you can bring me something very special for Christmas this year. I have waited 12 long months to ask you this. All I want from you is a letter from Billy. You see, Billy is my older brother. He was 16, and he died last Christmas from something called cancer. I don't know what that is, but it made him really sick and mommy and daddy have been very sad since he went away. I hear them fight all the time lately. Daddy said to mommy that he doesn't know why Billy went to heaven, but I know he's gone with the angels and I know that you must know where he is as you are all the way up at the North Pole. Billy was really funny and he used to tickle and play with me all the time. If you talk to him, can you let him know that I want to hear from him for Christmas and if not, tell him

I said hello and I love him. You don't have to bring me anything else, Santa, just a letter from Billy. I love you and your little elves. Also, Santa, please make mommy and daddy stop fighting, it hurts my ears.

Love,
Becky

Dear Santa:

After helping Becky with her Christmas wish, I found this poem that she wrote for Billy. I sat and cried for an hour after she left to go home. Innocence is so beautiful at so young an age, don't you think?

Love,
Aunt Violet

Billy

Billy used to tickle me
He always made me smile
He used to kiss me on the cheek
He made my life worthwhile
But now he's gone and the fun has
stopped
He is with me no more
He is now tickling little kids in heaven
He has gone through another door
Soon one day we will meet again
I will kiss him on his cheek
And he will tickle me again
When once again we meet
- Becky

* * * * * * * * * * * * * * * * * *

Dear Santa:

While cleaning up Becky's room last night while she slept, I came across this letter to you. I have read it at least ten times and sat down and cried another ten. After showing it to my husband, Bill, we both cried and thought how lucky we were to have such a beautiful daughter and though only nine, it seems a very wise one beyond her years. I will have to hug Aunt Violet when I see her next. You see when Billy Jr. died from cancer a few weeks before last Christmas, Bill and I died too. We started to fight about very foolish things and it took a little girl with a big, big heart to show us how wrong we were. We not only questioned our faith, our belief in God, and everything else, but our love for each other as well. No more! We both sat down and had a long talk last night and because of the insight of our dear little daughter we see how wrong we were.

When she gets up on Christmas morning, there will be a letter from Billy to tell her that he is fine and he will one day see her again. I will save this letter forever and will show it to her when she becomes a married woman with kids of her own. So many times in life we lose sight of the *real* spirit of Christmas and it takes the ideas of a little child to put everything back in perspective. We start to blame others when things go wrong and never once give thanks to a higher power for the things we have. Bill and I had to tell you this story too, so thanks for listening Santa and may your Christmas be made as bright as ours because of the love of our little nine- year -old girl.

Yes, there really is a Santa Claus,
- Becky's Mom

- RJH

Candy Cane Kisses

For you I have a candy cane
My darling little Miss
Is there something in return
Perhaps a sugar kiss?

At Christmas this was often said
To me by dear old Dad
He liked to spoil me rotten
Gave me everything he had

Although I loved those candy canes
Of which I was quite fond
Something meant much more to me;
Our solid loving bond

Every year when Christmas comes,
I have lots of candy canes
My love of this sweet peppermint
Brings me joy that still remains

Now I'm grown and Dad is gone
Though I have Christmas wishes
One would be to have him back
And give him candy kisses

Lisa J. Ivany

DUSTIN'S CHRISTMAS SPIRIT
(By Lisa J. Ivany)

The 23rd of December was just another long day for Dustin Broderick. His teacher had given him a book report to do nearly a week ago about the spirit of Christmas and he had yet to write anything on the subject. *Book reports - what a waste of time*! Dustin thought. To make matters worse, his five-year-old brother, Tyler, kept asking his mom about the Christmas spirit which repeatedly prompted Cheryl Broderick to ask Dustin if he had written anything yet. Little brothers, they always got you in trouble!

"Mom, what is the Christmas Spirit?" Tyler asked. "Is it an old ghost who haunts people's houses at Christmas?"

Dustin, feeling superior at the age of ten, laughed at his brother's question and said, "Tyler, don't you know anything about Christmas? It's all about getting games and toys under the tree on Christmas morning. The more you get, the better the Christmas spirit."

"That's not right, Dustin," his mother admonished. "The spirit of Christmas is in the giving and helping of others and not what you receive as gifts. It is also spending time with family and friends which gives you a wonderful feeling called the Christmas spirit."

"Yeah, whatever," he replied while rolling his eyes. Dustin didn't think much of his mother's version of the topic. He just wanted to get his book report done before he returned to school after the holidays.

"If you wanted to show some Christmas spirit, why don't you go across the road and shovel old Mr. Anstey's driveway," she suggested.

"I can't do that right now, mom. I have too much to do before Christmas," he said as he brushed by her to his room. He sat on his bed, counting the money from his bank that he had been saving all year from his recycling practice. Dustin lived in Back Harbour and had been collecting recyclable plastic containers from his neighbors here and also many residents of Twillingate and trading them in for cash. He had quite a little business going and his regular customers had their bags of bottles for him to collect every Friday after school.

Dustin had already bought Tyler's present weeks ago when he saw his little brother eyeing a brown teddy bear with a blue jacket and matching hat. For his dad, he had bought a special edition neon green measuring tape. Now, the only gift left on his list was a pair of navy suede gloves at Manuel's store that he saw his mother admiring just yesterday. Satisfied he had counted out over double the amount of money he needed, he whizzed out of the house to go shopping.

When he sped out of his driveway, he noticed Mr. Anstey toiling with his snow-filled shovel. He could hear the strenuous gasps for breath as the frail old man heaved each load to the side of the road. Dustin thought his elderly neighbor would surely collapse at any moment from the strain which seemed to be too much for him. He knew Mr. Anstey had terrible asthma and thought this couldn't be good for his condition. His shopping would have to wait.

"Hi, Mr. Anstey," Dustin called.

"Hello there, Dustin," the old man responded, pausing in his chore. "Are you all excited about Christmas?"

"I guess so. I'd be more excited if I didn't have to write a book report during Christmas break though."

"I'm sure you'll do fine," he laughed.

"Mr. Anstey, would it be okay if I finished shoveling your driveway?" Dustin asked.

"I'm sure you have better things to do today."

"No ... I really like shoveling," he coaxed.

"Alright, if you insist. I won't say no twice," he relented. "Thank you, young man."

For the next hour, Dustin studiously cleared Mr. Anstey's driveway and then placed the shovel in his shed. He looked at his watch and noticed it was lunchtime and he had worked up quite an appetite. He could taste the fries at RJ's Restaurant already. He was halfway down the road, when his mother called out for him to return.

When he arrived at the door, she said, "Come in and get your lunch. After that, I need to you look after Tyler for a couple of hours while your father and I visit your Aunt Millie in the hospital."

"Oh, mom! Do I have to?" Dustin protested. "I was just going to RJ's for lunch."

"Well, you can take Tyler with you."

"Oh Boy! Oh Boy! Oh Boy!" Tyler exclaimed behind his mother. "Are we really going to RJ's?"

Dustin saw the look of excitement in his brother's eyes and felt a pang of guilt for not wanting him to come along. With a complete change of heart, he smiled at his brother and said, "Come along, squirt. There's a burger at RJ's with your name on it."

Mrs. Broderick said, "Wait a second while I get some money for you."

"It's my treat, mom," Dustin replied.

The two boys dashed down the lane, stopping intermittently to make snowballs to throw at nearby trees or boulders. The air had a bit of a nip to it, but the boys were bundled up warmly in their snow suits, mittens, and caps. A few strands of golden hair peeked out from beneath their caps, flicking across their foreheads. The brothers were very similar in looks with their blue-gray eyes, long silky black lashes, dimples, and now even their rosy red cheeks matched.

The boys scampered to a table at the back of the restaurant overlooking the harbour. Even though it was winter and the water was covered in ice, they still preferred to look out the window at the bay. Dustin enjoyed the Christmas atmosphere in the festively decorated diner and soon after being seated, he looked through the glass and saw big fluffy snowflakes beginning to fall. Certainly, Tyler's singing "Here Comes Santa Claus" along with the radio heightened his holiday mood as well.

After stuffing themselves on burgers and fries, the two boys trekked off to Manuel's store to purchase the gloves for their mother. Dustin selected just the right pair and had enough money left after the purchase to buy Tyler a rubber ball he had been playing with in the store.

Dustin was surprised at how much he enjoyed the company of his little brother today. He wasn't such a nuisance after all, he thought. They pranced along the route home, sliding down snow banks and playing tag. As they rounded the top of the hill near their home, they fell in step beside Flora Watkins, pulling a load of wood on a sled. Dustin immediately came to her aid and helped her pull the heavy cargo. He knew she must be cold because of the old tattered coat she wore and her bare hands looked red from the cold.

Flora lived three houses down the road from the Brodericks in a run down shack that she kept heated with a wood stove. She was only in her 30's, but had been a widow for several years, after a drowning accident claimed the life of her husband. Since then, she had never remarried and had to cut her own wood on a daily basis and do all the other chores her husband had previously taken care of. She had no family in the area so there was no one to come and help her out when needed. She could not afford a better home on the low wages she took in from babysitting and couldn't even afford to replace the lock on her front door which no longer worked. However, there was no fear of anything being stolen from her home because she had nothing worth taking.

"Thanks for the hand," Flora said as they arrived at her door.

"Any time you need help, just ask me," he replied.

He went inside and stowed away the wood near the stove with the aid of his brother. Dustin had never been inside Flora's home before and was shocked at the sparse furnishings. There was an old rickety sofa with stuffing protruding in several places, cardboard boxes turned upside down to use as a coffee table, end tables, and even a larger one for a kitchen table, and two old spindly wooden chairs in the kitchen that looked ready to split in two. There were no electronics anywhere such as a TV, stereo, or computer, all of which Dustin took for granted on a daily basis. She didn't even have a Christmas tree! He was totally amazed how little this woman had and realized how comfortable he had it at his own home.

Christmas morning was a joyous event in the

Broderick household, until Dustin passed along the small wrapped package he had for his mother. He felt she would be disappointed when she opened it and found the message inside that read, "I.O.U." He wondered if she would be upset at not getting an actual gift, however, she smiled and hugged her son.

"What is the I.O.U. for?" she asked him.

"It's for a pair of gloves when I save up enough money to get them."

A rapping sound interrupted any further explanation as Mrs. Broderick left to answer the door. Flora Watkins stood in the doorway and asked to speak to Dustin. She was ushered into the living room.

"Hi Dustin," Flora began. "I don't know how to thank you for the beautiful gloves."

"You're welcome," he stammered. He felt terrible that his mother was now finding out he had given a gift to someone else and had nothing for her.

Flora looked at Cheryl and continued, "You have the most wonderful son. When I came back from gathering wood this morning, there was a decorated Christmas tree in my home and this pair of gloves wrapped up underneath it. There was no tag, but I knew who they were from because I saw them in the package your son was carrying yesterday."

Cheryl wrapped her arms around her son and said, "I'm so proud of you."

"You mean, you're not mad because I didn't give you the gloves?" he asked.

"Of course not. I think they look much better on Flora anyway," she answered graciously.

"Thank you so much again, Dustin," Flora responded. "You truly have the spirit of Christmas in you."

Cheryl turned to her son and said, "You should have no problem writing your book report now."

"What do you mean, mom?" he asked.

"Just write about your own experiences. I saw you shovel the driveway for Mr. Anstey yesterday, then you treated Tyler to lunch at RJ's, and to top it off you gave Flora a Christmas tree and gloves to keep her hands warm. You should have no problem writing your report."

"Hey, you're right, mom," Dustin agreed as he bounded up the stairs to get started on his paper. He was surprised to find that he was actually looking forward to it.

- LJI

ONLY ONE HEARTBEAT
(By: Robert J. Hunt)

The bubbles moved slowly up towards the top of the room. Multi-coloured, large and small, all shapes and sizes of the soap floated above the young couple lying in the bed giggling and rampant with excitement. The only light shining in the dim room was a small night light with open slits of stars and different coloured windows cut in unison around the lamp shade. The light of the bulbs illuminated the stars to make it seem as if the bubbles were indeed many different colours.

"Brad, you're amazing! How did you ever know that this coloured lamp shade would make this happen to the bubbles?" Cindy Johnson asked in amazement between quick bouts of laughter. Brad, her companion, shifted his weight on the bed and dipped the bubble maker into the soapy water and blew another round of bubbles into the air.

"Elementary, my dear Miss Johnson. I told you I'm brilliant," Brad kidded her as the bubbles cascaded off the bubble maker and drifted slowly towards the ceiling.

Over the past two years, Cindy had never laughed as much. She had come to the Janeway

Children's Hospital in St. John's with an erratic heart-beat that had to be monitored every day. The doctors told her and her mother, Carrie, that she would soon have to have a possible heart transplant as she had a tear in the aorta that would need attention in the near future. This was the reason she had to constantly be taken to the hospital to have it checked.

Brad Scott, who was the same age as Cindy at 16, had become her best friend over the past few years. He was diagnosed with leukemia two years ago and had been back and forth to the Janeway several times this past year.

As they lay side-by-side on the bed laughing and talking, their troubles seemed so far away. Brad was fun to be with, Cindy thought, and she hoped he would be her friend forever. But as of today, Dr. Chapman had some news for her and her mom and although she hoped it would be good, the glum look on her mother's face yesterday went against this.

"Got to go, Brad," Cindy huffed as she nudged her friend in the ribs and jumped off the bed, leaving him with slippery soap all over him. "Mom and I have a meeting with Dr. Chapman in half an hour. I'll talk to you after it's over."

Cindy exited the room, leaving Brad alone on the bed staring in space with his thoughts. One more month, possibly two, and the laughter would be no more. Dr. Cummings had broken the news to his mom, dad, and family a few days ago. The leukemia had started to enter its final stages. The news was over-whelming to all and Brad knew his time was short. He had yet to find a way to tell Cindy that every day he was getting weaker and weaker.

A few doors down the hallway, Cindy sat with her mother. Carrie's husband had passed away several years before and Cindy was all she had to live for now.

They sat facing Dr. Chapman to hear what he had in store for Cindy.

"The problem you have been having since you were ten years old can be corrected by surgery, but not properly," he said. "We can operate and repair the tear in your heart, but it will eventually open again as you grow older, making for more troubles in the future. The only way to ensure that you will lead a normal life, Cindy, is to have a transplant. From what we can gather, this will allow you to lead a normal, healthy life. The main concern is to find a proper donor and to have this done, hopefully, before Christmas."

Over the next few days Brad and Cindy spent a great deal of quality time in each other's company. As Cindy took antibiotics to become stronger, Brad's strength was beginning to weaken quite noticeably, but that never stopped his sense of humor.

"Cindy, the St. John's Maple Leafs will be in town in another few weeks so I'll have to pick up some tickets for the next game. I'd write a cheque for you if I wasn't so tired." He winked at her for approval.

"No problem, Brad. I'll see what I can do. Just leave the cheque on the table for me tomorrow." She turned her head as Brad drifted off to sleep and her eyes became moist. How would she be when the time came for Brad to slip into endless sleep? She couldn't answer her own question with the lump in her throat.

A few days later, Brad took a turn for the worse. His parents were called to the hospital and he was given his last rites. On a Wednesday morning he had stopped being administered Morphine for pain and passed away with his family, Cindy, and her mother at his side.

His last words were for Cindy. "I'll be there with you at the game, Cindy." When these words were spoken, he closed his eyes for the last time.

About an hour later, while Brad's family, Cindy,

and Carrie were still grieving at his bedside, a light knock sounded at the door. Dr. Chapman poked his head through the door and said, "Excuse me for intruding at such a difficult time, but I need to speak to you and time is of the essence."

After being ushered in by the Scotts, Dr. Chapman continued, "Last Saturday when I was doing my evening rounds, your son asked me for a favor."

"A favor?" Mrs. Scott questioned. "Brad didn't mention this to me."

"Actually, it was his last request that he wanted granted after he passed away. He said you didn't like talking about his impending death which is why he came to me," Dr. Chapman counseled. "He said he wanted his heart to go to Cindy when he died so that she could enjoy a long and happy life. We've run the appropriate tests and it looks like Cindy would be an excellent candidate for your son's heart. However, it's up to you to decide whether to donate Brad's heart or not. I know it's a big decision which you'd like to think about, but the heart can only be sustained a few short hours after death so we will need your decision over the next couple of hours and, of course, Cindy's approval."

In Cindy's saddened eyes a flicker of hope surfaced. She looked at Dr. Chapman and before anyone spoke, she said, "I would be honored." Turning to Brad's parents, she implored, "Mr. and Mrs. Scott, to have Brad's heart beating in my body would be a privilege. I loved him so much and this way a part of him will always be with me. Please say yes and I promise to take very good care of his heart."

Sobbing openly, Mrs. Scott embraced Cindy and with an affirmative nod from her husband, she responded, "Yes, of course. You've become like a daughter to us and we know how much Brad adored you. Knowing the best part of Brad is living on through you will make our loss more bearable."

Dr. Chapman pulled an envelope from his Lab coat pocket and said, "I must present this letter before we prepare for surgery. A few days ago, when Brad was feeling very weak, he asked me to write this letter for him. It was the hardest thing I've ever had to do. It's addressed to you, Mrs. Johnson, and he asked that you read it to everyone in this room when he passed away." He handed the letter to Carrie.

With shaking fingers, she gently slit open the envelope and extracted the paper inside. She slowly unfolded the letter and read:

Dear family and Cindy,

I now know that it is only a matter of days before the Man above comes to claim what is rightfully His. All the wishes in the world cannot stop this. So, instead of trying to ask Dr. Chapman and God for the impossible, I want to pass my wish on to Cindy.

Cindy, take my heart for your very own. Make it only one heartbeat for the both of us. Walk in the snow this Christmas and know I will be there with you. Touch the trees that I cannot touch. Feel what I can never feel again, let the breeze blow through your hair, and know that I am there beside you. May my heart beat in you until you are 90 years old and when your time comes, I will take you by the hand to join me. You will be alive tomorrow and I will be alive inside you, always. I love you, Cindy. I love all of you.

Brad

Upon completion of this reading, not a dry eye was seen in the hospital room. Composing himself, Dr. Chapman, approached Cindy and handed her another envelope from his breast pocket. He said, "Brad also asked me to give you this."

She extracted two tickets revealing the Mile One Stadium insignia, dated for February. There was a short note attached which read, "Enjoy the hockey game when you have recovered. They are the best seats in the house for you and me, Cindy."

- RJH

(In memory of Ben Ivany; one terrific dad.)

WINKING LIGHT
(By Lisa J. Ivany)

Each December in Gander, I would be found following dad and his ladder through the snow from one end of the house to the other. As he tacked the Christmas lights in place along the eave, through the trees, and around the railing, I would insist on replacing non-functioning bulbs and passing along tools as he needed them. This was our yearly ritual and although neither one of us enjoyed being out in the cold, it was a special father-daughter bonding time.

I remember one year, after we had strung the lights and put the ladder away, a bright yellow light, at the highest point of the eave, would go out for a few seconds and then come back on for a few seconds. This was repeated several times and I reported it to dad, who in turn went out and changed it with a new bulb. That seemed to work just fine and I went out to a party and forgot about it.

On returning home later that night, I noticed the

same pattern of blinking coming from the same socket as before even though it had been replaced with the new bulb. I entered the house and found dad sitting in the living room.

"Dad," I said. "The same yellow light is blinking again."

"Okay, my darling, I'll replace it tomorrow."

The following day dad went out to change the light, but it was no longer flashing so he left it as it was. All through that evening there were no problems with the outdoor lights and the yellow bulb continued to shine steadily. In the evening, I again went out to another Christmas party and arrived home late. On my way up the driveway, I noticed the yellow light back to its previous blinking habit.

Once inside the house, I went in search of dad to tell him of the problematic bulb. I found him in the kitchen, sneaking a late-night snack. I crept up quietly behind him as he was bent down, gathering goodies from the fridge.

When I was just inches away, I said loudly, "Back away from the fridge!" Immediately, he jumped in surprise, almost toppling the plate in his hand.

"Oh my God!" he exclaimed. "I thought you were your mother."

"Don't worry, Dad. I won't squeal on you," I laughed. "I just wanted to let you know our yellow bulb is out there flash dancing again. Maybe you should try replacing it again tomorrow, even if it isn't blinking when you look at it."

"Lisa, my dear, I think there's a reason that bulb only flashes at night when you come home and that you're the only one who sees it."

"Why's that, dad?" I asked.

With a teasing grin, he said, "I think it's actually the ghost of Christmas Past, signaling that you are home safe and sound. Perhaps the light is not blinking at you, but rather, *winking* at you. The ghost probably has a crush on you."

"Oh, dad," I said in feigned exasperation. "I think mom must have put too much rum in that fruit-cake you're eating." I kissed him goodnight and went off to bed with the sounds of his amused giggling in the background.

Oddly enough, for several Christmases after that there would be a flashing light in the same spot of the house every year, even though the lights were never strung in the same order. Of course, dad would repeat his theory of the ghost of Christmas Past to friends and family, even to the point where people started believing him because I was the only one who had ever seen it.

One Christmas Eve when dad and I were wrapping presents in the kitchen, he brought up the ghost story again and embellished it a bit further by saying, "One day, when I'm no longer here, I'll have to get rid of the ghost of Christmas Past and find another light to wink so you'll know I'm watching over you. I'll choose a different spot on the house, perhaps lower, so you can see it easily without having to look up too far. Maybe over the garage door."

"Dad, you are so silly sometimes," I retorted. "Besides, you're going to live forever." How could I have known how soon those words would return to haunt me.

Three months later, my father passed away very unexpectedly and my comfortable and serene world was forever changed. Somehow life went on, but things were never the same in a world without the kind and gentle nature of Ben Ivany.

When the following Christmas approached, I didn't have the heart the string the lights without dad, but my brother was kind enough to take this task out of my hands.

After leaving church from the midnight service on Christmas Eve, I returned home with my mother to spend our first Christmas without dad. A few moments after being inside, I realized I had left my hand bag in the car and went out to retrieve it. On my way back to the house, my attention was drawn to a single *winking* yellow light above the garage door. The usual flashing light at the top of the house from previous years was glowing bright and steady. For a moment, I was paralyzed by the remembrance of the words dad had spoken to me on his last Christmas. This astonishment turned to a sense of comfort when I realized who was winking at me and I winked back.

Now, when I see a winking light, I know it's from the ghost of Christmas Present as dad continues to watch over me.

- LJI

CHRISTMAS TRIVIA

Candy Cane Legend

If you turn a candy cane upside down, it reveals the letter "J" which stands for Jesus. The hard white peppermint symbolizes the solid rock foundation which the church was built on.

Then we come to the stripes - the three narrow red stripes represent the lashes Jesus endured on the cross. The thicker red stripe is symbolic of the blood He shed for us all.

The next time you bite into a candy cane, remember, you are consuming a piece of Christmas history

North Pole

Have you ever wondered why Santa Claus decided to settle down to live in the North Pole? Well, actually, this decision was made by an American cartoonist by the name of Thomas Nast. In 1882, Nast portrayed Santa on top of a crate bearing the label, "Christmas box 1882, St. Nicholas, North Pole." This version became popular and several years later another artist showed Santa returning to his home in the North Pole.

Perhaps what inspired Nast to give Santa this remote residence is due to a portrait painted of Santa Claus by Clement C. Moore in "A Visit From St. Nicholas" where he is wearing a fur robe. This would mean he came from a cold climate. At that time, no one had reached the North Pole and many expeditions had failed. This remote and mysterious place seemed the perfect location for the magical Santa Claus.

NOTE FROM SANTA
(By Robert J. Hunt)

At this time of year, Christmas was very good for Sam. He made a lot of money and was very good at his craft. Why not? He had been taught by the best ... and then the rich fools, from whose houses he robbed never knew what hit them because he was in and out as quiet as Santa Claus. This comparison made him laugh to himself. Yes, he was good ... really good. For the seven years since he had been a thief, he had never even come close to being caught. Perfection. That's what he was! Samuel Michael Donovan; no friends, no one who cared for him. Nothing. Just another guy who could blend in anywhere ... and did. Of course, it wasn't always that way.

Seven years ago, he had a good job as a lawyer, a fine home, and lots of the good things in life. Then there was Paula and Amy, his wife and daughter. Things were perfect until it happened! Both were killed by a drunk businessman as he was leaving a party on Christmas Eve. They were killed instantly while Mr. Stiles, the man who had struck them, walked away from the crash with only a few minor abrasions. Oh, he received six years in prison and died while inside of a heart attack during his incarceration, but that wasn't enough for Sam. He was still bitter. While Mr. Stiles did his time, Sam, one night in a vengeful rage, broke into his mansion and stole everything in sight. The net gain ... over $140,000. It was two years after he was sentenced and Sam wasn't even questioned about the incident. That began his easy life of break and entry.

In seven years he had broken into over 50 homes in different cities, all lavish homes as Mr. Stiles' home was and now had amassed a fortune of over $3,000,000. Sometimes he hit a small home just for the fun of it, to keep sharp. Now, as he surveyed the small home of Ms. Young, well, it was too good an opportunity to pass up. A single woman living by herself as far as he could see. The old man must have left her a bundle when he died or left her. This would be too easy! She left the house at the same time every night and didn't return until 3:00 the following morning. In and out, God they made it so easy!

The next evening, Sam arrived at Ms. Young's house just as she was leaving with her little girl. Little girl! Looks a little like Amy. But where did she come from? Sam hadn't seen a little girl when he had scouted the house this past week.

What is she doing? Sam wondered, as he saw Ms. Young help the little girl into the van. He couldn't make out what was happening as the van obscured the view. So, she has a little girl, big deal.

Sam waited in the car as the van drove away and night fell. He waited another hour and surveyed the house once again, got out, and slipped into the bushes behind the home. One quick look around, up to the back door, sized up the lock, and he started to work on it. Two minutes later he was inside. He'd start with the bedrooms first. Up the stairs he went in the well- decorated home.

Kind of reminds me of my own home from years ago, Sam thought.

Into the first room on top of the stairs he crept. What he saw made him shiver slightly. He had entered the little girl's room. In it he found all the things that young girls collect and his mind raced back to Amy's room and his heart nearly stopped when he saw the crutches leaning against the wall.

God, the child must be crippled, he thought.

That's how Amy was born, with a bone defect that made her wear crutches to strengthen her legs until she was to reach 15 and have an operation to fix them, the operation she never received.

Sam had to leave the room. Something was happening to him that had not happened in years. He quickly walked out of the room and as he headed down the hallway, something told him to go into the mother's room. He entered and spied a letter on the table that he guessed was written by Mrs. Young. He picked it up and read:

Dear Santa,

My little girl, Amanda, asked me a few days ago if I had written to you yet. I lied to her and said I did. Then, today, I felt guilty and decided to write this letter, I guess, as a way of expressing how I feel. So bear with me while I explain the hurt I have inside.

You see, my husband, John, died last year on Christmas Eve when he was killed by a drunk driver on his way home from work. I was devastated for I loved him so much. Amanda has a rare bone disease where she needs several operations to correct the problem and John did not have enough insurance to cover all the expenses. He left us with the home, but little more. Right now, I need $100,000 to make my little girl whole again. If you send it to me ... well, you under-

stand what I'm saying and it will renew not only my faith in God, but my faith in you as well.

I have to leave now to bring Amanda to a specialist in another city for more tests. Thanks for listening to the tears of a mom who would do anything in this world to make her daughter whole again. Merry Christmas.

Mrs. Terry Young

Sam couldn't believe what he was reading! Husband killed in a car accident, little girl crippled ... it was an exact carbon copy of his life or what had happened to him years ago. Sam sat on the bed and the emotions of his wife and daughter overtook him and he wept openly. He made a pact to himself that this would not happen to Mrs. Young nor to Amanda. He may not be able to change the past, but he sure could change the future. He took out a pen and paper and began to write,

Dear Mrs. Young,

I have read your letter with great interest. I have devoted my life to making people happy and to make them believe I am who I say I am. Because of the situation you find yourself in and the faith and love you hold for your little girl, you will have the money sent to you within three days of reading this letter. To this, you have my solemn word and promise.

May your daughter find the same faith in her later years as you have now. I wish for you and Amanda the merriest of Christmases.

Truly,
Santa Claus

Sam went back to Mrs. Young's room, searched and found her bank deposit book, noted the number on it, and left the room. He smiled as he read the letter again, picked up his knapsack, and walked down the stairs and out of the house to his car. He turned once more and felt the most wonderful feeling he had in several years. He smiled and nodded towards the home.

"Thank you, Mrs. Young and Santa, for renewing my faith in all that is good," he said as he slowly drove away from the home. He made a mental note to make sure Mrs. Young received her money in three days plus a lot more so that Amanda could have all that he had lost. He also made a pact with himself to start a new life filled with hope and kindness to all.

- RJH

LOVE IS BLIND
(By Lisa J. Ivany)

Repetitive explosions of gunfire boomed in the distance on that gray December day. It was close enough that the makeshift Army Hospital's walls shook with each blast as it struck earth, machines, and man. Although most of the staff and wounded soldiers seemed oblivious to the war raging outside, Drake Peddle lay on his cot reliving his own war-oriented nightmares. His sightless hazel eyes remained open and his body so motionless that one might mistake him for a corpse. Short black wavy hair surrounded a ruggedly masculine face and matched the thin mustache growing on his upper lip. It suited him and seemed to detract from his slightly elongated nose.

His mind raced as he torturously endured end-less replays of his last battle. Try as he might, he could not get the horrid images out of his mind of his com-rades, who had become like brothers to him, each being cut down in a series of blasts from grenades, torpedoes, and gunfire. Once again, in his darkened world, he saw his best friend, Austin Bailey, collapsing to the ground as a bullet pierced his left kneecap. Drake ran to his friend's aid just as the earth exploded before him and everything went black. That's the point where the images stopped for a moment until his brain rewound events and the re-enactment started again.

In Drake's 30 years he had never had a better friend than Austin. Although similar in their tall, broad stature, Austin's eyes were pale blue and his hair was as blonde as Drake's was black. They did everything together from the time they started Kindergarten, in the historic community of Trinity in Newfoundland's beautiful Trinity Bay, up to adulthood. They even enlisted to fight the war in the Middle East and as luck should have it, managed to be in the same platoon. On the fateful day that took Drake's sight and the use of Austin's leg, the two friends shared accommodations on adjacent cots.

"Hey Drake," Austin called out in his usual chipper fashion. "You awake?"

"Yeah."

"A letter just came for you." He paused, wondering if he should even have mentioned it to his pal. "It's from Emma."

"It's been nearly a month this time," Drake said. "I guess it's getting harder to get the mail through the closer we get to the front lines."

Austin asked, "Do you want me to read it to you?"

"Maybe later. I'm feeling tired right now."

"Alright, buddy. I'll just head on down to the Lounge and show Nurse Finlay how she and I can both fit in this wheelchair," he laughed and sped down the corridor.

The images of death and destruction were then converted to more painful images as Drake reflected on the beautiful face of the woman he would never be able to see again. Emma Hiscock, two years Drake's junior, lived in nearby Port Rexton and had captured his heart at a high school dance. They had been inseparable ever since.

He pictured her when he left her at the dock, tears streaming from her sad green eyes while the blustering wind whipped long golden tresses about her oval face. Clad in only a faded denim jumper and mint green tee shirt, he still thought she was the prettiest angel this side of Heaven.

It was a cool April day with a gale blowing over the water, stirring up white-crested waves and teetering the vessel haphazardly in its berth. Emma waved to him as he boarded the ship, touched her fingers to her shapely plum-shaded lips, and blew softly to deliver a delicate windswept kiss before he sailed away. She then clasped her fingers around the engagement ring Drake had given her the previous evening with a promise that they would marry when he returned from the war.

However, everything was changed in the blink of an eye or, more appropriately, in the blast of a grenade. The doctors were not hopeful of his ever regaining his sight and he would not expect Emma to be burdened with his affliction for the rest of her life. She had her whole life ahead of her and deserved a whole man, he thought. With this in mind, he mailed a letter to Emma a fortnight ago, penned by Austin as Drake dictated. It read ...

My Dearest Emma,

I hope all is well with you and your family. Please send them my regards. I imagine you are still longing for this war to be over and for my return home. Well, that's why I'm writing, Emma. I will not be returning home after the war. I will be going to a special training centre in Ontario.

I've been thinking about you a lot and although I love you, I just don't want to be married. I guess I've gotten used to living on my own since my parents died and would find it hard to adjust to having someone else around all the time. I hope you understand and I'm sorry if this hurts you. However, I'd rather tell you now than keep you hoping for something that's never going to happen.

Please keep the ring as a reminder of happier times. Try to go on with your life as quickly as possible and I hope one day you will be able to forgive me.

Love, Drake.

He hated lying to her, but knew if he told her the truth, she would adamantly refuse to break the engagement. Her deep sense of duty would bind her to him forever and he knew in time he would be a heavy chain around her neck, weighing her down.

Well, at least the part about going to a special training centre was true. Of course, he wouldn't tell Emma it was an educational centre for the blind. The facility was located in Hamilton, Ontario and Austin agreed to fly there with Drake in the new year to get him settled into the facility. Austin would then return to Trinity with the sworn oath to Drake that he would not tell Emma about his condition or where exactly in Ontario he was located.

"Hey, buddy!" Austin yelled as he screeched to a halt at Drake's bedside, but not quite quick enough to avoid hitting the side rail. "We're sprung out of this Hell Hole!"

"What are you talking about?" Drake asked.

"I just got the word from an especially friendly Nurse Finlay that you and I will be discharged on December 19," Austin announced. "That's tomorrow!"

"I guess that means we'll be in Trinity longer than expected," Drake mused. The original plan was that they would be released after Christmas which would give him a couple of days to pack up his belongings at home and go to Ontario. He wanted to get in and out of the bay as quickly as possible to avoid any contact with Emma. Now, he would be trapped there longer. However, he thought, it would be a relatively minor risk after the letter he had sent to her. Anyway, he'd probably be there and gone before she found out.

"Drake, do you want me to read Emma's letter now?" Austin asked.

"Yeah, I guess so."

Austin read ...

Dearest Drake,

I haven't heard from you in a while and trust you are keeping safe. I hope this war is over soon and that you will never have to be put in danger again.

It is with a sad heart that I write this letter and I know it will cause you grievous pain, however, I cannot keep you believing we will be together after the war. You see, I have met someone else and although I have remained faithful to you until now, my feelings for this other man have become too strong to deny. I'm sorry I must tell you this in a letter, but I thought you deserved to know the truth instead of expecting a future together.

I hope you will find somebody new and perhaps with time you will learn to forgive me. Take care of yourself and stay safe.

Love, Emma

Drake sat in silence a few moments, absorbing the letter's contents. Then he said, "Well, I guess I don't have to worry about how my letter is going to affect her after all."

"I'm sorry," Austin replied. "I wish I hadn't been so eager to read it to you."

"That's okay, my friend. I guess this eases the guilt about my own letter now," Drake said. "I'm glad she has moved on with her life and I hope she's happy."

Boxing Day in Trinity began with heavy snowfall and gusts of wind spitting out blankets of white powder throughout the community. Visibility was virtually nil and most people stayed inside rather than risk Mother Nature's wrath. As most Newfoundlanders know, the weather can change in five minutes and four seasons can be experienced in one day. That Boxing Day was no exception with the sun's bright energetic rays in the afternoon and by evening a sky peppered with millions of sparkling stars. The air was calm, the snow crunched underfoot as mummers scurried from house-to-house, and the smell of wood stoves filled the air.

Inside his white with black-trimmed two-storey home, Drake was reclined in a chair by his fireplace. He listened to Bing Crosby singing "White Christmas" as he toasted his stockinged feet near the fire. He joined Bing in singing the well known carol and thought back to the previous Christmas when he had his sight and the woman he loved.

The front door slammed shut, followed by the thump of boots being thrown into the corner of the porch. Roused from his senseless memories, Drake heard the heavy-footed steps combined with the thud of a cane as Austin sauntered down the hallway. He was happy his friend had graduated from a wheelchair to a cane so quickly. Certainly, Austin's enthusiasm for life would never keep him down for long. Drake sometimes wished he had the same positive outlook.

"Hey, Austin. I'm by the fire," he yelled.

Settling himself on the sofa, Austin didn't waste time on pleasantries. He began, "Have you heard the news about Emma?"

"What news?" Drake asked as a lump formed in his stomach. "Did she get married?"

"No. At least I don't think so," Austin added. "I

meant the news about her face."

"What about her face?"

"Well, apparently the fish plant in Dunfield where Emma was working was turned into a temporary canning factory while we were away. They can foods there to send over to the Middle East to feed our troops. Apparently there was an accident where one of the cables snapped from the machine Emma was working on." He paused for a moment before delivering his next words. "I was told that it sliced down the whole side of her face."

"How bad is it?"

"No one really seems to know because she keeps it hidden under a black scarf all the time. Some kids are starting to call her the Scarf Lady."

"Come on, Austin!" Drake exclaimed as he jumped to his feet. "I need you to be my eyes."

After driving his friend to Port Rexton, leading him up the front steps, and rapping loudly on the door, Austin left his friend on the stoop.

After what seemed an interminable time, Drake heard the latch turn and the door slowly opened. He could not see the woman whose face was half hidden by a black scarf, but he did hear the sharp intake of breath, revealing that he had startled her.

"Drake! What a surprise! Come in," she said.

While stepping aside to allow him entry, she noted the walking stick and sunglasses. She asked, "Is there a problem with your eyesight?"

"If you consider being blind a problem, I guess so," he remarked.

"I'm so sorry, Drake. Why didn't you tell me?"

"Maybe the same reason you didn't tell me about your face."

He heard the tremor in her voice as she said, "I wanted to remember the way you looked at me when you thought I was beautiful. I couldn't bear the thought of seeing you look at me with revulsion or pity for the rest of my life. If you could see me now, you would probably turn your head in disgust. No man will ever want me now," she moaned.

"What about the man you told me about in your letter?"

"Drake, there was never any other man. You're the only one I've ever loved, but I didn't want you to stay with me out of a sense of duty."

"Did you think I was so shallow that I only loved you for your looks?" he accused. "Emma, it's what's inside of you that attracted me to you in the first place. I don't care what you look like and never did. It's your spirt and your soul that I'm in love with."

"I'm sorry, Drake. I should have had more faith in you ... and in us. I have always loved you and only you."

With these words, all the negative emotions Drake had experienced while lying in an Army Hospital in the Middle East for so many months came to a halt. He now knew that he wanted to spend the rest of his life with Emma, his soul mate. Though he could not physically see, he realized that his blindness was only an affliction for him, but would never be for Emma.

He paced back and forth, easily maneuvering his walking stick in the familiar living room he had so often visited before. He slowly walked towards Emma and reached for her hand. Clasping it tightly, he pulled her close, dropped the stick from his other hand, and slowly raised that hand to her face. She flinched as his fingers found the scarf and lowered it to her shoulders. He again reached his fingers to her face and tenderly caressed the jagged edges of damaged skin, following its entire course.

A smile crossed his face and he remarked,

"You're still the prettiest angel this side of Heaven." He leaned forward and without the aid of sight, adeptly guided his lips to hers. A flow of sweet emotions blazed through their hearts as love's remembered kiss was reunited.

With reluctance, Drake broke the kiss and said, "The whole time we were apart I thought of you night and day. Even after I lost my sight and my foolish pride composed that letter, your image was permanently etched in my mind and my heart."

"You may have lost your sight," she said, "but I'm the one who was blind."

The feel of his mouth reclaiming hers in a passionate kiss made her realize that it didn't matter. At that moment the war and Emma's accident both became distant memories.

- LJI

BILLY'S ANSWER (To Becky's Wish)
(By: Robert J. Hunt)

Becky snuggled in her bed as the light from the stars shone in through her window. She was so happy to go to bed every night this past week before Christmas as she knew that the small voice she was hearing at night was coming to her stronger and stronger with each passing day. She knew who was trying to talk to her.

She couldn't wait for bedtime to come so the voice would talk to her again. Maybe this Christmas Eve was the night when Billy would let her know that he was listening to her prayers. She told her mom and dad about the voices in her head, however, they said it was nice to have good dreams of him, but she was overreacting at this time of year. They felt it was because Billy had died a few weeks before Christmas the previous year, but Becky knew differently. She knew it was Billy talking to her.

* *

Billy was forlorn as he looked down at Becky. After her letter and poem last year, she had become so sad that he had left her and he knew that his troubled sister was starting to dream of him every night. His friends here had told him this would happen to one so young and that looking at his earthly sister would cause heartache for him.

Reading Becky's letter had made him sad in a place where sadness was no more. However, at this time of year they were given an opportunity to look at their earthly families and the lives they had left. He knew that he had to contact her though he knew it was not normal protocol for angels, but he had to ease Becky's mind concerning him.

* *

As Becky lay in bed, she said her prayers. She always saved her last for Billy so she could speak to him about the day she had. Lying there, she asked God to protect her mom and dad and one day see Billy again.

"Thank-you God, again, for making mommy and daddy stop fighting," she spoke. "And please let Billy know everything is okay and that I love him on this Christmas Eve."

She had just finished her thoughts when a soft, gentle breeze floated through the room and a sweet voice spoke to her.

"Why not tell Billy yourself?"

Becky turned her head to see an angel so beautiful it took her breath away.

"Wow! Are you really an angel?" Becky asked.

"Yes, Becky, I am," came the reply. "And I have someone here who wishes to say hello to you."

The angel stepped aside and behind her stood Billy.

Becky sat up straight in bed and smiled. She knew this was no dream, but rather, Billy keeping his promise of one day seeing her and talking to her.

"Hi, Billy," Becky said with mounting joy.

"Hi, little angel. I saw you so many times praying to me that I received special permission from my superiors to come and speak to you on this Christmas Eve night."

"Oh, Billy, I knew you would come! I'll go and get mommy and daddy."

"No, Becky," Billy interrupted. "It will do no good because only you can see me."

"But, Billy, how can I show them that I was speaking to you? When I told them I was doing so in the past few days, they said it was something they called over-reacting. What does that mean?"

"It means, Sis, that though you knew I was trying to contact you, they thought it was all in your mind." He paused a moment and continued, "I promise you I will leave them a sign to let them know that I have spoken to you."

"Okay, Billy. What do you want me to do?"

"I want you to write a letter to mom and dad for me and I will guide your hand across the paper to help you write it. Do you think you can help me do that?"

"Oh yes, Billy. I know I can and mommy and daddy will be so happy to know my dreams are not called over-reacting," Becky beamed.

Saying this, she got out of bed and went to her desk. Billy took her hand, selected a pencil, and began to write these words:

Dear Mom and Dad,

I know this will probably come as a shock to you both, but Becky is writing this special letter from me to you. I will only be given this chance once and have chosen this Christmas, one year after I left, to speak to you. So please know that it is really me as I will leave a sign with you by letter's end.

I am in a wonderful place of pure euphoria and there are no such words as sadness or pain. Everyone here is kind, gentle, innocent, and as pure as Becky. There is no hatred or anger; no sickness or cruelty. The kind souls here are all happy and the pain I felt before I passed away is no more. Know that here love is everlasting.

As I guide Becky's hand here tonight, I am so grateful to my Creator for giving me the chance to say how much I love you mom, dad, Becky, and Aunt Violet and how much I miss you. We will all be together one day and there will be happiness forever. I wish you all a very special Merry Christmas.

I love you all,

Billy

P.S. Mom, remember the time I broke your crystal kitten you loved so much, but you told dad you accidentally did it while dusting? Only you and I know this happened. I was only eight years old and Becky was just born.

Billy wrote his P.S., squeezed Becky's hand, leading her back to bed, and said, "I have to go Becky. I only have a few minutes before I return to my friends, but you take this to mom and dad in the morning. Tell them I love them and will be with you all in spirit on Christmas Day and always. I love you, Becky."

"I love you too, Billy," she said as deep sleep overtook her.

* *

Becky awoke at 5:30 on Christmas morning. She looked at the desk and saw the letter glowing and knew this Christmas would be very special. She jumped out of bed, gathered up the letter, and ran to her parents' room.

"Merry Christmas, mommy and daddy!" she said excitedly. "I have a very nice present for you this Christmas," she squealed as she passed her mother the letter. "See, I told you I was talking to Billy."

Her mother took the letter and began to read. Her heart felt as though it had jumped up to her throat as she read and re-read the letter over and over. "Oh, my God! Oh, my God! Bill, wake up!"

Her husband awoke with a start. He took the letter and as he read its contents, tears filled his eyes. He said, "My God, how can this be? How do we know this is not a fake and that it's not someone playing a cruel joke on all of us?"

She replied, "It can't be a joke, Bill. You see, only Billy and I knew about the crystal kitten he broke years ago. Also, that's Billy's handwriting. It has to be from him."

They gathered Becky in their arms and kissed her. She knew they would see Billy again one day and that he was in a place where he was very happy.

Downstairs, as Becky opened her stocking, Bill and his wife embraced on the sofa and thought about all the special miracles that happen at Christmas. They knew the letter was God's way of telling them that Billy Junior was safe with Him.

"We will never doubt you again, Becky," her mother said. "If you're ready, I think it's time we all opened our presents; you, me, daddy, and Billy."

Mom said a silent prayer, thanking God for the most wonderful Christmas present they had ever received.

- RJH

AN ELF IN HIDING
(By Lisa J. Ivany)

The North Pole workshop buzzed with activity on Christmas Eve as the elves quickly packed bundles of toys in a large red velvet sack for Santa's trip around the world. The little green-clad helpers were all excited about returning to their little snow huts to celebrate Christmas with their families. They would have a holiday break until after the new year when the toy-making process would resume in preparation for next Christmas.

As the last doll was wedged into Santa's hefty sack, the elves cheered for a job well done. The workshop door opened, blasting in cold winter air along with Santa. "Merry Christmas everyone. Is everything ready for my trip?"

"Yes, Santa," they all answered in unison.

He hefted the cinched bag upon his back and went to his sleigh. The elves donned their winter parkas before making their trek to Mrs. Claus' house for some eggnog before going home. The mood was jovial amongst the little toy makers, that is, except for Roper. Even though he looked forward to celebrating the season with his family, he still had a strong yearning to go with Santa on his trip tonight. He had heard about the children of the world, but had never seen one in all his 200 years. Roper was three feet tall and was fascinated to hear that there were many children who were actually taller than he though they were much younger. He longed to see one for himself, but there was a strict rule that no one was permitted to travel with Santa. Oh ... how he wished he could leave the North Pole, if only for a night.

The rest of the elves had already left the workshop to see Mrs. Claus when Roper was zipping up his jacket. As he turned to switch off the lights on his way through the doorway, he noticed something under the table. It was the baseball glove, autographed by Larry Walker, that nine-year-old Tommy Jennings wanted for Christmas. It must have fallen out of Santa's sack. Oh no! He must get this in the bag right away or Tommy would be terribly disappointed in the morning.

He sprinted across the thick blanket of crisp white snow to the sleigh, climbed into the back, and proceeded to untie the rope around the sack. After all, he didn't want the big guy to think the elves were incompetent by leaving toys behind. The shift of the sleigh indicated that Santa had just taken his seat up front. Then the familiar phrase rang out, *"On Dasher, On Dancer, On Prancer, and Vixen..."* Panic seized Roper as he tried unsuccessfully to untie the rope's knot. It was fastened so tightly his little fingers could not budge it. Intent on his futile task, he didn't hear Santa's final words, *"On Blitzen."* Whoosh ... Roper fell to the floor, still grasping the baseball glove, as the sleigh took flight.

The bells jingled on each reindeer harness as they leapt to the sky. The air was chilly with a sprinkling of thick fluffy snowflakes on this Christmas Eve. Santa called out, "See you in the morning Mrs. Claus," as he waved to his wife below. "Ho, Ho, Ho, Merry Christmas!"

Roper stayed huddled on the floor in the back seat, fearful Santa would discover him. He had never seen Santa angry before. In fact, Santa was the jolliest fellow he knew. However, no one had ever disobeyed Santa by riding in his sleigh. Would Santa be mad if he knew? Would he even believe him when he said he didn't intentionally stow away? After all, everyone knew Roper's biggest wish was to go on Santa's sleigh and meet a child some day.

Crouched in hiding, Roper was amazed at how swiftly Santa traveled around the world, briefly stopping at each rooftop and whipping through chimneys with lightning speed. Upon landing at each home, the sleigh's computerized travel log announced their destination and the names of the children within the house. Santa then grabbed his sack and easily popped his hefty frame down the narrow chimney opening.

Halfway through the night, Roper heard the computer say, "32 Snowden Street, Roddickton, Newfoundland ... home of Tommy and Susie Jennings." Roper was still clutching the baseball glove and knew what he had to do. With his free hand, he clasped the end of one of the sack's ropes and held on tight. Roper was quickly airborne, clinging to the bag's cord, as Santa hoisted the sack up onto his back.

A brief moment of darkness enveloped the two travelers as they descended the chimney, followed by a low cast of light as they landed with a soft thud below. Roper scurried behind a nearby chair to remain hidden. He watched in awe as presents magically flew out of the sack and settled under the tree while the jolly man snacked on cookies and milk. As Santa nibbled his treats, Roper silently slid under the chair and guided the baseball glove into a position behind the tree without being seen.

Roper studied his surroundings, delighted by the

festive atmosphere. Multi-coloured streamers hung from the ceiling, extending across the living room, a country village adorned the mantelpiece with a blanket of artificial snow, and the pine-scented tree loomed in the corner in gargantuan proportions. At least, to some-one of Roper's stature, it appeared huge. On an oval cof-fee table in the center of the room a tantalizing display of assorted snacks was a welcoming sight. Propped against the sofa lay two bulging stockings with the names "Tommy" and "Susie" embroidered in red let-ters.

Oh No! Roper had not seen Santa finish filling the stockings. Wild-eyed he scanned the room, but there was no sign of Santa! He had heard stories of how quickly and quietly the man in red worked, but he never imagined it would be in the blink of an eye. Bong! Bong! Bong! Roper nearly leapt out of his skin as the grandfa-ther clock chimed the early hour of 3:00 a.m. What was he going to do now that Santa had left him behind in Newfoundland? What if he was discovered by one of the natives? He had never met anyone outside the North Pole and wondered if Newfoundlanders were naughty or nice.

"Are you a real elf?" a voice exclaimed behind Roper.

He froze in his tracks, too terrified to move.

Again, the voice asked, "Hey, are you a real elf?"

Roper slowly turned around and looked up into the face of a boy. He certainly didn't look threatening even though he was taller, but the hammering of Roper's heart intensified. His answer came out in a gasp, "Y-eee-sss," he stammered.

"Wow!" I've always wanted to meet an elf," he giggled.

Roper, started to relax and asked, "Are you Tommy?"

"Yes and I bet your name is Roper."

Shocked, Roper responded, "How did you know that?"

"It's written across your cap."

"Oh yeah," he laughed. "I guess that was pretty obvious."

Tommy sat on the floor in cross-legged fashion to enjoy the company of his new companion. He wore Spider Man pajamas and his sandy blonde hair was disheveled from the tossing and turning he had endured earlier in the night. Although excited about meeting a genuine elf, Tommy's sleepiness showed in the drooping of his eyelids. With balled fists, he continually rubbed his weary eyes in an effort to stay awake.

"Shouldn't you be in bed asleep?" Roper asked.

"It's Christmas Eve!" Tommy exclaimed. "This is the hardest night of the year to sleep."

"Yeah, I guess you're right. I always find it hard to sleep on this night, too."

"Wanna play *Galactic Gliders*?" Tommy asked.

"What's that?"

"It's my newest video game and it's totally awesome!" Tommy replied as he switched on the television set. He retrieved two hand sets and plopped down next to Roper in front of the TV screen. He handed one device to Roper and explained the rules of the game.

An hour later, amid empty milk glasses and plates lined with cookie crumbs, the two players finished their competition, with Roper the ultimate victor. In all fairness, Roper thought Tommy probably let him win. He looked over at his new friend to see if he wanted a rematch, however, Tommy had succumbed to exhaustion and now lay on the floor fast asleep.

"Wake up sleepy head," Susie Jennings yelled at her brother.

Tommy abruptly awoke, a little disoriented at

first, until he focused on the faces of his parents and little sister. He then realized he must have fallen asleep in the living room while playing with Roper. He jumped up and scanned the room, but his new friend was gone. He asked, "Did anyone see Roper?"

"Who's Roper?" Susie asked.

"He's the elf who came here last night with Santa."

"Really!" Susie squealed in pure delight.

"Now, Tommy, don't go telling your sister tales," Mrs. Jennings reproached. "I'm sure there was no elf here."

"But, mom," Tommy started, before his mother cut him off.

"I'm sure you were so excited about Christmas that you dreamed you saw an elf. Everyone knows that elves never leave the North Pole."

Tommy saw the futility in arguing with his mother's logic. Perhaps he did dream the whole thing after all. Thoughts of Roper were put aside for the moment as he raced to open his stocking with Susie. He didn't even notice the puzzled look on his mother's face as she cleared away three empty milk glasses and found only a trace of crumbs from the mound of cookies put out for Santa the night before.

When Tommy reached for his last present, tucked back behind the tree, he shrieked in delight, "Wow! It's an autographed Larry Walker glove! I wanted this so much!"

His parents looked at one another questioningly. Mr. Jennings whispered to his wife, "I've tried for months to get that glove for Tommy, but could never get it. How did you manage to do it?"

"I didn't. I have no idea where it came from," she replied. She turned to her son and asked, "Who is it from, Tommy?"

"It's from Santa," he beamed. Under his breath he continued, "And Roper."

Meanwhile, at the North Pole, eight sets of reindeer hooves thumped down upon the snowy runway as the jingling sleigh landed. Roper sat up front with the big bearded man for the return trip. Santa had come to his rescue and quietly whisked him up through the chimney while Tommy lay sleeping.

The journey back was made in silence as Santa concentrated on operating the computerized craft. Roper didn't know how upset the big guy was with him for his little escapade to Newfoundland. He timidly mumbled an apology for causing trouble and jumped down from the sleigh.

"Roper, you do realize there are consequences for your actions, don't you?" Santa asked.

"Yes, sir."

"Well, first of all, you will have to unharness the reindeer and settle them into their loft. After that, I'd like you to clean up the workshop."

Upon completion of his chores in the reindeer loft, Roper headed for the workshop, wondering how much cleaning he would have to do. He flicked on the light switch which illuminated a very empty, but tidy room that had already been cleaned. It had a strange aura of stillness and peace that was very unusual in this place which was normally noisy with the sound of many elves crafting toys. He turned to leave and saw a note on the memo board addressed to him. It was Santa's handwriting and the message said ...

Roper,

I know the reason you were on my sleigh tonight. If not for your kind heart, Tommy would not be enjoying his baseball glove at this moment. I told you there are consequences for your actions which is why I purposefully left you behind at Tommy's house. I knew you wanted to meet a child and since Tommy wanted to meet an elf, I thought I'd combine the two Christmas wishes into one. Ho, Ho, Ho. Merry Christmas, my friend.

Santa

Roper raced down the lane to his snow hut, jumping and skipping in glee while feather-soft snowflakes tickled his face. His heart soared as his Christmas wish had come true and Santa was not angry with him. This Christmas was the best one yet.

After removing his outerwear and settling on the sofa, Roper spotted a shiny red package beneath his tree. The tag said, "To Roper From Santa." He tore off the paper excitedly to reveal a *Galactic Gliders* game. He wasted no time connecting his new toy to his television set. When he was about to press play, a rapping sounded on his door. He wondered who it could be, but did not want to pull himself away from his new game.

"Come in," he called out.

The door thudded closed, followed by footsteps striding down the hallway. "Can I play too?" a voice asked.

"Of course and I'll even let you go first," Roper offered as he handed an extra remote to his guest. "Thanks for this great game, Santa, and especially for the trip tonight."

"You're welcome, Roper, but you can thank me by letting me win," Santa joked as his belly shook with mirth.

- LJI

My Christmas Angel

I look up at an angel
As I lay in this withered state
Snowflakes melt on the window
So close to heaven's gate

My pain is somewhat lessened
As I stare at this Christmas tree
A hospital bed can be lonely
But this angel will comfort me

I know my time draws near
But the Lord will have to wait
"Little Drummer Boy" is playing
My favorite carol on this date

This Christmas Eve may be my last
As I gaze toward the sky
I have made my peace with God
Peace made before I die

I'll take His hand in comfort
As He stands here by my side
With my Christmas angel beside me
He will always be my guide

Robert J. Hunt

A MISSION OF LOVE
(By Robert J. Hunt)

There was only one woman he had ever truly loved, but Brent had never told her and for many years he regretted not doing so. Over time, he had let distance separate them and so they had drifted apart, but perhaps it was for the best. Now, nearly eight years had passed since he had seen her, but that did not erase his thoughts of her. As a matter of fact, he thought of her nearly every day since he had left home. Somehow, when he thought he was safe with his thoughts, she crept into his mind from out of nowhere. He saw her as he always did, her light-platinum blonde hair, dark complexion, light-hazel eyes and perfect smile. *Why had he not asked her to marry him eight years ago? But to give her what ... this kind of life?* he thought. This life was not for her. His life involved going all over the world to assist World Youth in its quest to conquer world hunger. He sat with his feelings and wondered what she was doing at this precise moment home in Buchans, Newfoundland, a week from Christmas day. She was six thousand miles away and his heart still ached for her after all these years.

Brent Holwell snapped back to reality at the sound of young voices as a calloused hand touched his shoulder. Two children from the village were speaking, asking him to come outside. He splashed cold water on his face and told them he would be only a moment. He put his memories back into seclusion and wandered toward the door of his bamboo hut. Brent was now a missionary in Kadome, Zimbabwe and had devoted his life in pursuit of helping others in Third World countries that so many other nations had all but forgotten about. He immersed himself into his mission in life to forget his past of mental abuse from his father and his death, his mothers's early passing, and the love of his life, Dawn Gibbons. Brent exited the small hut that housed him and his fellow workers. Nearby, speaking to a group of tribe elders was Trevor Parker, the mission's leader and his good friend. He finished speaking to the group and approached Brent.

"Brent, How are you doing this morning?" he asked

"I'm fine, Trevor, and you?"

Trevor gave him that big wide grin that he was famous for and asked him to come sit with him. Brent complied and sat next to Trevor on a make-shift wooden bench.

"Brent, I have some good news for you, my man. In two days' time, I am happy to say, you will have completed your eight year term here is Nascarie Settlement and will have some leave coming to you," he informed his friend. "My request to you is that you take it and go home to Newfoundland for awhile. God knows you deserve it after all the work you have put in here. I'd also advise you to consider the newly vacated position in the Newfoundland office to oversee World Youth's efforts.

Brent looked at his friend and knew that this was

coming as he had refused leave several other times over the years to stay behind with his friends and devote his time to the poorest of the poor. But longing for home and Newfoundland had become stronger and stronger and, of course, there was Dawn. He then knew what his reply to his friend would be.

"Trevor, I have been here for years now and have seen much suffering and misery. I'll go home in the hope of raising some much needed funds for the settlement. There's also some unfinished business I need to take care of in Buchans," he added under his breath. "However, I don't think I'll take the posting back home. I have a feeling there is no reason for me to stay there anymore."

Two days later, Brent said goodbye to his missionary friends and was on a 16 hour flight to Toronto and then from there to Newfoundland. After half a day's journey, he landed in Gander International Airport and rented a car for his drive to Buchans. On arrival, he was amazed how little it had changed over the years. He spent most of the day visiting friends and thinking how he would approach speaking to Dawn when he saw her. Someone said she had moved over by the new Redwood Lake district on the outskirts of town. He was hoping to see her as he walked through town and thought of an accidental meeting, but this did not transpire on his rounds. As darkness fell, he decided to walk the mile or so to her home with the hope of being lucky enough to catch her out walking. As he approached Dawn's home, he marveled at the way it was prepared for Christmas and how it gave the impression of a happy home. The lawn was decorated with Santa, his elves, and the reindeer. The home shone with a multitude of color as lights twinkled brightly amid the softly falling snow.

He started slowly up the walkway to her home,

but stopped suddenly and stared at the partial view he had through the front window. From the obscured angle he noticed a man, around his age of forty, talking to someone in the room. He took a deep breath and reeled back so as not to be seen. *My God! She's married!* he thought and his heart nearly stopped. *I'm years too late. I should have realized that someone as beautiful as Dawn would be married by now.* His heart was very heavy as he stared, transfixed to the spot. How foolish of me to think she would still be free. He adjusted his position outside the window and saw Dawn sitting by the fireplace with her hands folded on her lap. Brent's first reaction was how beautiful she looked siting there. When he could bear it no more, he turned and walked away.

Dawn's father, Angus, was just getting up from his nap. He stretched and walked to open the window to get a breath of cool, fresh air. He looked out into the night and was amazed to find a young man standing in the shadows looking into the front window of his home. There was something vaguely familiar about him. *No, it couldn't be!* he thought as the stranger started to walk away from the house. *Surely it was not Brent Holwell! Was he not away somewhere in Africa or some other foreign country doing missionary work? Where is he going? Is he not going to come in?* Angus grabbed his coat and raced down the stairs in pursuit of the figure. Opening the front door, he rushed after the stranger a short distance ahead of him .

"Wait! Wait!" he sang out again.

Brent slowed at the sound of a voice calling to him. As Angus approached, Brent nodded his head in acknowledgment.

"I thought that was you, Brent. My God! How have you been all these years?"

Brent turned fully, staring at the home, and shook his hand warmly.

"Hello, Angus, how have you been, my friend?"

"Brent, why did you walk all the way out here, stop by the front door, and not come in to see us? I'm sure Dawn would love too see you. Please, come back and join us."

"I don't know, Angus. I thought maybe after all this time it was best to leave things as they were."

"Nonsense, please come back with me." He took Brent's arm and led him back toward the house.

Brent nervously accepted his arm and proceeded back to the house with Angus clutching him. Upon arrival at the front door, the man that Brent had seen through the window was standing in the doorway. Angus stopped by the door and introduced them to each other.

"Brent, this is George Gibbons, my brother's son, who is home on leave from the Army for Christmas. He just dropped by to say hello and to wish us a Merry Christmas. Come on inside and see everyone and chat for a while.

Brent allowed himself to be towed by Angus inside the house. *Maybe she isn't married after all!* Brent thought. His heart leaped back into place as he followed them both into the foyer. Angus called to his wife, Paula, and Dawn to come see a visitor whom they had not seen in a long while. Both came around the corner from the dining room and stood looking at Brent in total shock! Dawn's stare showed that she was in total disbelief.

"Brent, I can't believe it is you after all these years."

She walked forward, hugged him, and kissed him gently on the cheek. Silence followed and for a few awkward moments both stared at each other intently. Angus turned to his wife and George and said quietly. "Come on you two. I think Brent and Dawn need to speak to one another."

They left the room, leaving Brent and Dawn alone. Finally, after what seemed an eternity, the silence was broken by Dawn.

"Brent, after all these years of wondering where you were, I had just about given up hope of ever seeing you again," she said.

With his head slightly turned, he said to her in a low voice, "Dawn, please can you ever forgive me? I have thought of you many times over the past years and when we parted, you moved away for awhile without any contact. I thought you didn't want me in your life so I followed my second love and became a missionary. I know that this will sound lame, but I never stopped thinking about you or what you were doing. After all these years I gave up as I thought you were, indeed, married. The main reason I returned home was to see if this was true."

Dawn stared at him as tears began to form in her eyes.

"Brent. I did move away years ago, but I never married. I became pregnant and now have a son, Rory. But I didn't want his father to give up his dreams that he had all of his life, so instead of marrying him I left so he could make his decisions and achieve them without any problems."

"Whoever this man is, he is very lucky to have you do this for him." Brent said.

" I don't know about lucky for I haven't seen his father for many years," she said. After a slight uncertain pause, she continued, "You see, Brent, Rory is your son!"

The words hit him like lightning striking a tree. His knees became weak and he had to sit down. He wanted to speak, but nothing came out. *His son! It couldn't be!*

"My God, Dawn, are you serious? I have a son! Why didn't you tell me this long ago? You know I would not have left if you had done so."

"Brent, I knew in my heart and soul that you wanted to be a missionary, for I have never seen anyone so dedicated to helping others as you. But I also knew that you couldn't bring a child up in such horrid conditions so when I became pregnant, I decided to go away so you could follow your dream. I realized later what a terrible mistake I had made, but we didn't know where you were gone or what organization you were with."

Brent replied, "I have thought about you every day for the past eight years and if you will permit me, I would like to see you and Rory for the next eighty years.

"I'd like that, too," she smiled, slipping into his awaiting embrace.

A few moments later, they entered Rory's room and watched as he lay peacefully sleeping. Brent leaned over and kissed his son's cheek for the first time and knew he had come home to stay.

- RJH

LETTING GO
(By Lisa J. Ivany)

"Stephen, for the last time, quit slurping your tea," Aunt Penney scolded. "You're 15 so start acting your age."

"Alright, alright, relax," he replied in exasperation.

"Penney, it's Christmas Eve. Can't you show the boy some Christmas spirit?" Bruce asked his wife. "Let's enjoy our dinner and forget about table etiquette tonight."

"You're right, Bruce. I shouldn't have snapped like that," Penney apologized. Turning to Stephen, she said, "I'm sorry."

Stephen wondered why Aunt Penney was so agitated today. She had been bordering on hostile ever since she picked up the mail this morning. In fact, she had secreted herself away in her bedroom shortly after sorting through the flyers and cards, most of which were left behind on the telephone table. However, he did notice the way she nervously clutched one particular gray envelope before leaving the room. He wondered if something in that correspondence caused his aunt's apprehensive mood. He decided he must read the contents of that letter.

"Oh my! Look at the time!" Penney exclaimed. "Bruce we've got to get moving if we're going to get all these presents delivered before Midnight Mass."

"I'll wash and dry the dishes so you can get an early start," Stephen offered. He was thinking ... the sooner he got them out of the house, the sooner he could search for the letter. He adored his aunt and hated seeing her so upset. Since he left St. Andrew's nearly 10 years earlier to move in with his Aunt Penney and Uncle Bruce in Clarenville, Stephen Tucker had been treated with warmth and kindness. His aunt and uncle were unable to have children of their own and thought of Stephen as a son.

He kept a photo of his mother on his bedside table although he would not have needed one to remember how she looked, for Penney Greening was his mother's identical twin sister. They both had long, curly strawberry-blonde hair flowing around heart-shaped faces with sapphire eyes, thin pert noses, and well defined lips that melted hearts with every smile. That was before his mother passed away on New Year's Eve all those years ago. Sadness tugged at his heart as he thought of the anniversary of her death drawing near.

Stephen, himself, had dark brooding eyes with straight coal black hair. His light olive skin could be traced back to some Indian lineage on his father's side. Although he had no photo of his father and his aunt refused to speak of him, on occasion an old colleague of his father's would visit and remark how much Stephen looked like his father. Up until he was incarcerated, Joseph Tucker was a well respected anaesthesiologist and many old colleagues still admired the man.

"We'll see you later tonight," his aunt called over her shoulder. Stephen had been holding the front door open while his aunt and uncle edged through the opening with arms piled high with an array of brightly wrapped packages.

After placing the last dried dish in the cupboard, Stephen sprinted down the hallway to his aunt and uncle's bedroom. He knew what he was about to do was wrong, but he thought if he knew the reason for his aunt's agitation, maybe he could find a way to help. He opened the night table where they kept all their correspondence and rifled through the envelopes, ensuring he kept them in the proper order. At the very back, he found the gray envelope he sought and extracted the letter. It was from Dorchester Penitentiary in Nova Scotia and the note was short and to the point. It stated, "Please be advised that inmate, Joseph Tucker, has been granted parole. He will be released from prison on December 22 of this year."

Stephen gasped in shock! Now he knew why his aunt had been so uneasy. The man who had murdered her sister (and his mother) was now free! He stared at the paper with mixed emotions. He had many happy childhood memories of camping and swimming with his dad in the summertime and ice fishing and skating in the winter. However, they soon dissipated as he remembered the rage of losing his mother and then his father being sent to prison for killing her. He could not let go of the anger inside; not only for his father ending the life of his beloved mother, but for causing him to lose both parents and ending their idyllic life.

Stephen's anger burned hot inside as he made his annual trek to the local Roman Catholic church at 9:30 p.m. He chose this particular time each year so he would be alone between services. He didn't attend Midnight Mass, preferring his own private ceremony to honor his mother. He had been coming here to light a candle and say a prayer in her memory on Christmas Eve since he arrived in Clarenville as a boy. He knew she was watching him from above and he wanted to let her know she was remembered at Christmas.

The church was quiet at this time of night with a peaceful aura in the dimly lit parish. He walked to the table at the back of the church and lit a candle for his mom from the flame of another. A liquified pearl of wax glided down one side of the taper as though mimicking the tear slowly descending down Stephen's cheek. He wiped it away, crossed himself, and then approached the front of the church where he sat in a pew near the altar. He bowed his head and prayed. He hoped once again that he would be heard by his mother and by God. When his prayer ended, he raised his head and opened his eyes to look at the glittering golden cross on the wall behind the pulpit.

"Hello, Stephen," a voice whispered.

Startled, he jumped in his seat, thinking God had spoken to him!

"I didn't mean to scare you," the voice said.

Stephen turned and looked into a pair of bespectacled dark sorrowful eyes. A handsome man with a thick swatch of dark hair laced with gray and a beard to match sat in the pew behind him. He smiled at Stephen through lips etched in sadness, as though this was an unfamiliar expression for him.

"How do you know my name?" Stephen asked the stranger.

"I'd never forget my son's name," Joe Tucker responded.

Stephen sat in stunned silence a moment. He stared intently at the man, looking for some clue to substantiate his claim. Could this really be his father? He hadn't seen him since he was five years old and the man he remembered was clean-shaven with pure black hair and didn't wear glasses. However, a person could change a lot in ten years and this man's eyes were like a reflection of his own.

"If you *are* my father, you should know I want nothing to do with you," Stephen snarled.

Joe Tucker pulled a wallet from his coat pocket and extracted a plastic photo sleeve. He passed it along to his son and said, "Look at the photos inside and you will know I am your father."

Stephen flipped through the photos which revealed his yearly school pictures, including his most recent grade 10 photo. At the very back was a wedding photo of his parents. How happy they looked, he thought.

"Now do you believe me?" Joe asked.

"Yeah, but how did you get my school pictures? I'm sure Aunt Penney didn't send them to you."

"No, she didn't, but your Uncle Bruce did."

"That doesn't change the way I feel. You killed my mother and I'll never forgive you for that ... never!"

"You don't know the whole story, son. If you will hear me out, I'll explain the reason I took your mother's life."

"Forget it," Stephen snapped. "It won't bring her back." He bolted from his seat and sped down the aisle to the front door. He ignored his father's plea to stay and listen. The huge wooden door banged loudly and echoed throughout the rafters, leaving an eerie stillness in the boy's wake.

Joe hefted himself to a standing position with the aid of his cane. His limp was more pronounced in the cold winter months where arthritis had set into an old knee injury. It certainly would inhibit him from catching up to his son. He hobbled down the path his son had traversed moments before. Midway down the aisle, the door swung open as Stephen returned.

He stormed up to his father and exclaimed, "Actually, I would like to hear what you have to say! I want to know what possible reason you can give to justify killing my mother!"

"Son, as you probably know, your mother was very ill for a long time before she died. You must remember all the trips to the hospital in Port-aux-Basques to visit her." He watched as Stephen nodded his head in agreement before continuing. "She was dying from bone cancer and was in unbearable pain for the last few weeks of her life. She spent a horrible Christmas season in a hospital bed, pleading with me every day to let her go. By letting go, she meant for me to end her life."

A thick mist formed in Joe's eyes as he relieved the most difficult time in his life. Shifting his weight, he continued, "It broke my heart to see her in so much agony, but yet the selfish part of me didn't want to let her go. She begged me every day to end her life. Finally, on New Year's Eve I couldn't bear to watch her endure any more pain and granted her final wish as I administered a lethal injection to end her suffering."

Large droplets of tears splashed down Stephen's cheeks as the impact of his father's words sunk in. For all these years he had thought of his father as the villain when all along he was actually a man who loved his wife enough to help her die and spend ten long years in prison to grant her final wish.

The empty church reverberated with the sounds of father and son sobbing loudly as they embraced each other in their mutual grief and thus began the process of healing.

Stephen felt that an insurmountable weight had been lifted from his shoulders as he let go of his toxic anger. He may have lost his precious mother, but he had reclaimed a father on this wonderful Christmas Eve night.

- LJI

THE CROSS
(By Robert J. Hunt)

On this Christmas Eve, Adam Churchill sat in the church pew wishing he had not come here. He felt uncomfortable and nervous as his eyes scanned his surroundings. A slight chill crept up his spine. Whatever had possessed him to enter the Pentecostal Church in Lewisporte as he went about his Christmas routine, was surely beyond him. Adam had not been to church since his dad had passed away on Christmas Eve ten years earlier.
"I guess," Adam surmised, "something is telling me to remember dad by coming to church today."

Oh well, a few moments more and he'd be gone with no harm done. He'd say a small prayer for his father, on the anniversary of his death, and be on his way again.

As he looked about and his eyes became accustomed to the darkness, he became transfixed on the statue of the crucified Christ on the cross. He stared at this man with his head bowed, nailed arms outstretched and broken feet and thought how much He must have suffered in the events leading to his deception, capture, and ultimate crucifixion. Adam reached out and lightly touched the statue's feet. A shudder went through him.

His mind flashed back to his own dad and how he saw how much he had suffered years before his death. Cancer had taken him away at only forty-eight years of age. Adam recalled this as he sat thinking and in his mind saw again the terrible and dishonorable pain his father had endured up to his death on Christmas Eve so many years ago. Isn't it amazing how one thinks and sees things as they sit in church by themselves?

As he sat, he said a small prayer for his dad and his mind raced back to good times they both had shared........the laughter and joking they both enjoyed......as fathers and sons do when together. He thought how his dad had shown him right from wrong, how to be humble, how to be good to people and how to have love and respect for God. Also, how to be a man! As he sat thinking, Adam also felt ashamed! His dad had taught him about commitments and inner peace they both had shared that he somehow now had left behind. Adam blamed God for his father's death and felt embarrassed looking up at the man on the cross.

The cross.......Adam remembered the cross his father had always worn around his neck. He remembered how his dad loved it and spoke of it with pride and heart-warming adoration.

"It is my rock," Adam had recalled he had said. He now felt ashamed that he had desecrated his father's memory by not coming to church for so many years.

I wonder whatever happened to dad's cross, he thought. *I'll search for it when I return home this evening.*

Adam felt a cold wind creep behind him again. It was as if the church door had been open and a wayward wind had passed into the church unescorted. As the chill slowly evaporated, Adam once again looked toward the cross of Christ to say goodbye and make a promise to God and his dad to come back to church from this day on. He paid his final respects to the crucifix, asked God's forgiveness, genuflected, and walked outside into the cool night air.

"Can you help out a poor man at this time of year, sir?" Adam was startled as the voice broke his thoughts. He looked at the poor vagabond and skeleton of a man with tattered clothes from head to toe. Immediately Adam's heart went out to this unfortunate soul. He took twenty dollars out of his wallet.

"Sure, my friend, here you go and Merry Christmas to you."

Though his face was not exposed, the stranger smiled and unexpectedly hugged Adam to show his appreciation for his kindness.

"Thank you, kind sir, may we cross paths again in the future," he exclaimed, turned, and went on his way.

Suddenly, a warmth came over Adam that he hadn't experienced in a long, long time. At that moment he felt as if his dad had been the one who touched him moments ago. Adam felt like a newborn as he drove home. He felt as if the weight of the world had been released from his heart. All tension and pressure left him as if he were weightless. He was indeed humble and at peace with himself. He made a mental note to search the house from top to bottom and not stop until he found his dad's crucifix.

Quite a day, Adam thought to himself as he entered his home that he and his parents had lived in all their lives. His mom kissed him on the cheek as he entered the house and helped him remove his topcoat. When his coat was put away, his mom screamed at him as he turned around.

"My God, Adam, where have you been?"

Adam looked at her with a bewildered stare.

"Mom, the strangest thing happened to me today. I went to church and spoke to God on the cross.

It seemed like dad was sitting next to me as I spoke to Him."

"My dear God! Adam please go and look at yourself in the mirror," she exclaimed with a puzzled look on her face.

Adam walked to the hall mirror and stared in disbelief at what he saw! Around his neck hung the cross his father so dearly loved!

"Dear God, how did this happen? This is impossible! I haven't seen this cross for years and I'm sure I didn't put it around my neck this morning."

Then he remembered the old man whom he had seen outside the church and given the money to. He then knew that his father had made sure that his cross, that had been lost for years, was returned to him.

"This year, mom," he said as he hugged her, "dad will surely be with us for Christmas."

- RJH

CHRISTMAS TRIVIA

Christmas Bells:

There is a legend that the first Christmas bell was heard by a blind boy. Apparently, a large group of shepherds were making a journey to Bethlehem in hopes of seeing the newborn king. A little blind boy heard the rumors and asked if he could go with them. However, they didn't want to be bothered with the child and left him behind.

After the shepherds had gone and everything was quiet, the boy heard a cow's bell in the distance. Believing the cow to be in the stable where Jesus lay, he followed the sound and it led him to the holy manger.

Tinsel:

When Mary and Joseph were fleeing Herod, they came upon a cave in which to hide. At night, while they slept, a spider covered the cave's entrance with cobwebs and the approaching soldiers did not bother to look inside.

The next morning Mary and Joseph were amazed at how beautifully the cobwebs glittered in the sunlight. Since that day, tinsel has been used on Christmas trees to symbolize the webs that saved Mary and Joseph.

Another tinsel legend tells of a visit the baby Jesus made to homes one Christmas Eve to bless Christmas trees. In one home he found the tree covered in cobwebs and when he blessed the tree, the cobwebs were transformed into strings of gold and silver.

LUCKY'S SURPRISE
(By Lisa J. Ivany)

"I'd like to be in Hawaii now," Lucky Summers moaned, brushing a thick layer of snow from her crimson parka, scattering a white mist to the floor of the foyer. On removing her snow-crusted cap, thick brunette curls bounced down below her shoulders. "I hate snow and wish I didn't have to see another flake of it for the rest of my life."

"It wouldn't be Christmas without snow," Morgan laughed.

"I'd rather be lying on a tropical beach with sand scrunching between my toes," she purred. "Wouldn't you like to tear yourself away from working at the dockyard and escape to the sun for a while?"

"I must admit the thought of you in a string bikini does conjure up quite a pleasant image," he teased while slowly gliding his eyes over her lithe figure. He thought she was the most beautiful specimen God had ever created and felt so fortunate to have met her on December 27 the previous year. That was the day Lucky had turned 30 and Morgan Canning was asked to come along to a surprise party some friends and coworkers from the Battery Hotel had thrown for her. It was love at first sight and nearly a year later neither could imagine life without the other.

"I think I better join *Curves* again after Christmas," Lucky said as they walked to the living area in her home on Farrell Drive. "I feel winded after that walk. Either the streets in Mount Pearl are getting steeper or I'm getting more out of shape."

"You're probably just getting too old to keep up with me," Morgan joked.

Lucky playfully flicked his arm and mischievously batted her big sea-blue eyes at him, stating, "In case you've forgotten, you're a month older than me."

"Yeah, but I have more stamina," he grinned.

His infectious smile always warmed Lucky's heart and now was no exception. She graciously let his last jibe go unanswered, preferring to watch as he lit the log in the fireplace. His hazel eyes sparkled from the ignited flames and the glow of the fire bathed his ruggedly handsome face in soft tones beneath his short black hair. He oozed masculinity from every pore and as Lucky stared at him from across the room, she felt her given name denoted the way she felt.

Tomorrow would be their first Christmas Day together and Lucky was looking forward to opening her presents with Morgan in the morning and then they were going to Torbay in the evening to have dinner with her family. She imagined their joyous faces when she exhibited a diamond on her left ring finger. She felt the butterflies resurfacing in her stomach at the thought.

Morgan had never mentioned getting married, however, Lucky's best friend, Abby Russell, seemed to think a wedding was in her near future. She had been in the Avalon Mall the previous week and saw Morgan leaving Charm Diamond Centre with a small package in his hand. She was so excited for her friend, she just couldn't keep it to herself and promptly mentioned the sighting to Lucky.

"I think we should open our presents tonight," Morgan said, breaking Lucky out of her trance. After lighting the fire and turning on the tree lights, he had quietly crept up behind her and wrapped his arms around her waist, snuggling his chin in the crook of her neck.

"It's not Christmas for a few more hours," she responded.

"That's close enough for me."

"No way. That would spoil the fun in the morning."

"Just one," he pleaded.

"Okay, but only one," she laughed. How could she say no, she thought, when he looked like he was about to burst with excitement. She remembered her father being the same way this time of year and realized that men were just oversized boys at Christmas.

After opening one of his gifts, Morgan turned to Lucky on the sofa and said, "Now, it's your turn."

She wondered if she should unwrap her gift from Morgan. She saw him place it under the tree earlier in the evening and although it wasn't the shape of a ring box, she thought he may have tried to disguise it. The box was short, slender, and wrapped in metallic red foil with a thick silver bow.

While she contemplated which present to choose, Morgan's enthusiasm overcame him and he picked up the shiny red package. He quickly handed it to Lucky and said, "Here, open this one."

With trembling fingers, she slowly slit open the paper. Her heart pounded rapidly, anticipating the ring soon to be on her finger. With bated breath, she extracted the box, flipped open its lid, and found an envelope inside. She knew this could not contain the jewel she desired. Disappointment flooded through her as she released the breath she didn't realize she had been holding. Within the envelope she found two airline tickets to Hawaii for the following July. Normally, she would have been ecstatic with this dream gift, however, she found herself mustering up an artificial smile for Morgan's benefit.

"Wow, this is fabulous!" she squealed in feigned delight.

"Then why don't you look excited?" he asked.

Covering up her lack of enthusiasm, she gave him a concentrated look and replied, "Well, there are two tickets here and I'm just wondering who I'll take with me."

Putting on a look of shock, he said, "Me, of course!"

"What if I decide to take one of my other boyfriends," she teased.

"Then I'll have to tickle you into submission," he warned. He flipped her down on the floor and repeatedly jabbed her sides, forcing her into hysterical laughter. He knew this was her weakness and she wouldn't be able to tolerate the torture for long.

After only a few seconds, she conceded defeat, saying "Okay, okay! You can have the other ticket. Just stop tickling me and let me up!"

"That's more like it," he beamed proudly.

Christmas morning, after finishing off her toast and hot chocolate, Lucky joined Morgan on the floor in front of the tree to open their presents. Her disappointment the previous evening had dimmed somewhat as she realized that it didn't matter if Morgan proposed or not because they were together and that's all that mattered. Abby probably misjudged what shop she saw Morgan emerge from. They cleared the paper debris from the room and snuggled on the sofa to watch Christmas cartoons on television. This was an annual tradition that they both never outgrew.

Halfway through the cartoon marathon, Morgan left for a moment and returned, holding a small wrapped package. He placed it in Lucky's hand and said, "I forgot about this last gift for you. I hope you like it."

Lucky's heart flip-flopped again as she looked at the tiny box in her hand. *Could it be the ring?* she wondered. She outwardly remained calm, but inside she was having a replay of the emotions she had experienced the previous evening. On removing the wrapping, emblazoned on the white box in gold lettering was the crest of Charm Diamond Centre. She realized Abby had been right about seeing Morgan there after all.

The smile wavered from Lucky's face as she withdrew a pair of heart-shaped diamond earrings. Once again, she quelled her true feelings and put on a pleasant smile.

"They're beautiful!" she exclaimed and wrapped her arms around his neck.

Morgan sensed Lucky wasn't as excited about the earrings as he thought she'd be and wondered why. First he noted the flicker of disappointment last night with the plane tickets and now he saw it once again. Before he could question her on it, she jumped off the couch and exclaimed, "Oh my, look at the time! We're going to be late for dinner if we don't leave now."

Lucky bolted to her bedroom to change before their drive to Torbay while Morgan went outside to warm up the car. She raced out the front door, still buttoning up her jacket as she scurried through the path to the car.

The tantalizing aroma of turkey welcomed Lucky and Morgan to the Summers' home and they arrived just as dinner was being served. Lucky was in high spirts, surrounded by her brother's and sister's families and Morgan was relieved to see her good-natured spirit back. Being with her family seemed to animate her to a higher level that Morgan envied. Being the only child, he never had the privilege of experiencing large family dinners and with his parents living so far away in Pasadena, he could not be with them on Christmas Day. The doctor had advised his father not to take long trips due to his failing health, but Morgan and Lucky had decided to go there and spend New Year's Day with them.

Two days later was Lucky's birthday, but she felt the most special part of the day was the fact that it was the first anniversary of when she had met the man of her dreams. The snow crunched underfoot as she and Morgan walked hand-in-hand through a trail in the forest. The sun was shining and the trees were laden with mounds of snow that sparkled as though sprinkled with thousands of miniature diamonds.

Although Lucky hated snow and the cold months of winter, somehow this year it all seemed more bearable. She found herself even liking the daily hikes on the snow-covered path and frequent barrage of flurries. She knew her sudden change in attitude wasn't due to an acceptance of Mother Nature's plans, but rather the contentedness she felt inside since Morgan entered her life.

Lucky's high spirits continued on into the evening as Morgan escorted her to a private suite he had booked at the Battery Hotel for her birthday dinner. After unlocking the door, Morgan stood back to allow Lucky to precede him into the room and then he flicked on the light switch. She gasped in awe at the suite filled with a multitude of coloured streamers, balloons, and birthday decorations. In the far corner next to the window stood a tall decorated tree with twinkling lights. Completing the ensemble was an elegant table set for two, displaying a red cloth, white candles, and champagne chilling in the decanter.

"Morgan, how did you manage to do all this?" she exclaimed.

"Actually, I can't take all the credit," he answered. "I just asked Abby to book the best suite on the top floor, overlooking the harbour, and she went into a decorating frenzy."

"Well, you've both gone to a lot of trouble for my birthday. Thank you so much," she said. "I should call Abby and thank her too."

"You can do that tomorrow. Right now we have a meal getting cold," he remarked as he pointed towards domed containers on the table.

After dining on French Onion soup and a scrumptious meal of breaded scallops, Morgan produced two slices of Chocolate Amaretto Cheesecake, Lucky's favorite dessert. In the centre of her slice was a single birthday candle which Morgan proceeded to light.

He said, "Now make a wish and blow out your candle, birthday girl."

She closed her eyes for a moment and then with a quick expulsion of breath, doused the flame.

"What did you wish for?" he asked.

"If I tell you, it won't come true."

"I don't believe that," he replied. "Furthermore, if you don't tell me, I'll have to get my tickling fingers in action."

"Oh no, not that!" she shrieked. "Okay, you win. My wish was to see your face across the table when I blow out my candles next year on my birthday."

"I have a feeling your wish will come true. Now, aren't you glad you shared that with me?" he laughed.

Morgan had forgotten about the time and took a quick glance at his watch. He noted the time was almost 10:00 and knew he had to time his next actions perfectly.

"Before we eat our dessert, why don't we let our

dinner settle?" Morgan suggested. "You can open your birthday gift now if you like." From beneath the table, he presented a wrapped package to Lucky.

She knew from the size and weight of the box that she would not be fooled this time into believing it was something from a jewelry store. However, she had made her peace with that notion and contentedly opened her gift. Inside the box was a pair of binoculars.

"They're great!" she said. "I can go bird watching in the summer."

"Actually, I thought you could use them for sightseeing when we go to Hawaii."

"Great idea," she beamed.

Morgan glanced at his watch once again and the time read 9:59. He propelled her towards the window and said, "Have a look at the harbour. It's all lit up for Christmas."

She looked down at the waterfront and the ships which were all displaying coloured lights from the first one to the last, all in a line.

"The lights are gorgeous!" Lucky exclaimed. "It's so nice how the coloured lights are on the outlines of the ships and there are small twinkling white lights strung in the centre of each, from mast to mast."

"Why don't you try out your binoculars and get a better look," Morgan urged. "I'll go and dim the lights so you can have the best view."

She raised the glasses to her eyes and peered down at the ships in the harbour. She gasped when she saw the white rope lights extending from the first vessel to the last! She blinked her eyes and adjusted the focus on the binoculars, but there it was again. The lights were twinkling in succession, spelling out the words, *Lucky, Will You Marry Me?*

She turned to tell Morgan what she was seeing, but he was on the floor, on bended knee, and extended a small velvet box to her. He raised it and slowly lifted back the lid to expose a sparkling diamond on a golden band.

He said, "Well, did you see my message out-side?"

"Ye-e-ss," she stammered in shock.

"Is that a "yes, you'll marry me" or "yes you saw the message?"

"Oh my God! I can't believe this is happening," she squealed. "Yes, I'll marry you. Yes! Yes! Yes!"

In her exuberance to hug him, she toppled him backwards onto the floor where she rained kisses upon him.

"I think it's time you let me up now so I can put the ring on your finger," Morgan laughed.

As he slipped the golden band on her out-stretched digit, happy tears trickled down her face.

"What's wrong?" he asked, confused.

"I'm just so happy that my birthday wish has come true. You will definitely be sitting across from me when I blow out my candles next year ... and every year after."

"That's a guarantee," he agreed. "And in case you haven't figured it out yet, we're going to Hawaii for our honeymoon."

An impish gleam covered her eyes as she responded, "Then I guess I really do have to give you the other ticket."

- LJI

THE LOTTERY
(By Robert J. Hunt)

He had played the same group of lottery numbers every week for nearly twenty years. They picked up tickets every Saturday and every other Wednesday night faithfully at Kelly's Shopping Mart in Bonavista. Jeff Hennessey was always thinking as others did about winning the Lottery and what riches could do for him and his family. However, for twenty years he was *always the bridesmaid, but never the bride*, so to speak. Twice he had five numbers that had won him $1,710 one time and then another when he had won $2,010 with some friends at work. But when reality set in, Jeff knew that winning it was the same as believing in Santa and then seeing him this Christmas!

All his working life, he and Tina, his wife of thirty-two years, had struggled to put their two children, Judy and Lucas, through high school and then university, which they did at the expense of draining their savings, but at least they both had graduated without owing any money for their education. Now that both kids were married with children of their own and had good jobs, he and Tina had set about paying off the $15,000 still remaining on their home. They had another $6,000 left to pay off their kids' education, $3,700 in incurred expenses in various other things, and the regu-

Svany & Hunt

lar cost of living. Such a simple thing as a vacation would be a thing of the past until these bills were paid in full.

Tina, at 57 years of age, recently retired form her job at the Post Office, but her pension plan only allotted her 65% of such a plan because she was never classified as a full-time employee. Jeff, at 58, would have loved to retire, but could ill-afford to do so. Living was comfortable, but not always easy as money always seemed to vanish. Both figured that they would be close to having all debts paid within another 6-7 years and only then could they think of retirement.

It was a week before Christmas and still all the gifts had not been bought. Jeff had a few more "surprises" to pick up for Tina and had one more payment at Crane's Jewelry for a special ring that she had long admired but never gotten because of its cost. Jeff didn't care about its $800.00 price tag, Tina was worth it and this year it was going to be hers! Many things went through Jeff's mind as he and Tina went about their last minute preparations for Christmas. Rush, Rush, Rush! This time of year there never seemed to be enough time to get all things done. Jeff had just started to put up the outside Christmas lights as Tina came rushing out through the front door.

"Got to go shopping, sweetheart," Tina shouted to Jeff as she walked to the car. "I have a million things to do today. I have to pick up dad and take him to hospital to check on his hip; I have to get Judy to help me shop for gifts for the ladies' bridge club; get some extra toys for the grandchildren; and several other things. I may be a bit late, so your supper is on the table and all you have to do is heat it up when you're finished stringing the lights."

Jeff barely acknowledged his wife as he became engrossed in an octopus of outside lights. Too many things to do and never enough time to do them, Jeff thought. Tina had just reached the car when Jeff shouted to her, "Tina, did you remember to take the Lottery numbers off the table for tonight's draw?"

"Yes, dear. I'll see you tonight." Tina called back to her husband before driving off.

Jeff spent over three hours putting up the outside house lights and then started doing the windows and decorating inside. After a few hours, his stomach growled. He looked at his watch and noted that it was nearly 7 o'clock. *Suppertime,* he said to himself and walked to the kitchen table. He put his lunch in the microwave and ten minutes later was enjoying his favorite meal ... Tina's fantastic fried chicken. When he finished supper, Jeff worked feverishly to have all the lights and decorations done before she arrived home.

Within a few hours, Jeff sat in his favorite chair admiring his handiwork and quickly fell fast asleep. At 11 o'clock, Tina arrived home and when she got out of the car, she admired the wonderful work that her husband had done on the house. *He had outdone himself this year,* she thought. She walked inside and marveled at his work and then noticed him asleep in the chair. *Poor dear, he's tired after all that work. I won't disturb him.* She covered her husband with a blanket, turned off the lights, and retired to bed to let Jeff sleep.

At 8 o'clock the next morning Jeff awakened to the stiffness that accompanies one who sleeps in a Lazy Boy chair for eight hours! Time for a nice breakfast before Tina awakens. *I'll make enough for us both and surprise her with breakfast in bed,* he thought. He washed and shaved quickly and proceeded to the kitchen to prepare bacon and eggs, juice, and cereal for them both. He turned on the television while cooking and within a few minutes the lottery numbers flashed up on the screen. It took a while for the numbers showing to register in Jeff's mind and he almost fainted! Oh, my God! I can't believe it! The numbers showing were not of first prize, but were definitely for the second winner and they were his! Jeff raced upstairs and burst into their bedroom. Tina awakened with a start. Jeff jumped on the bed and proceeded to sing Christmas carols while dancing up and down. Tina thought he was going crazy. After a few minutes, Jeff calmed and said to his wife, "Guess what? We just won second prize on last night's Lottery! I had the five correct numbers and the bonus number. That will put us in at least the $100,000 range." He continued to jump up and down on the bed, shouting and singing with glee. In a moment he noticed the shocked look on his wife's face.

"Oh, no, Tina, by the look on your face, please don't tell me you didn't buy the tickets. Do you remember me asking you to pick them up when you were getting into your car last night?"

Tina sat up straight in the bed, dumbfounded. She gasped, "Jeff, I thought that you were just saying that you would see me later on. I would love to tell you that I did get them, but the truth is, with so much to do I didn't realize what you were asking me when I was leaving."

"Are you sure, honey? Look in your purse even if it's just to humor me." Jeff pleaded.

"I'm sorry, dear, I would love to tell you that I did, but I would be lying because I didn't get them."

"Oh no!" Jeff said as they both sat down in total dejection. For half an hour they sat in stunned silence. Both didn't know what to say to the other. Finally, Jeff looked at his wife and said, "Don't blame yourself, honey ... it was totally my fault. I always pick them up a few days before Saturday and I should have gotten them before last night. What's done is done and we won't let it spoil our Christmas. The main thing is we have each other, our health, and the kids. Let's forget it and finish decorating."

"You're right, sweetie ... what's done is done," Tina acknowledged. "Let's not torture ourselves."

They went downstairs, enjoyed their breakfast together, and were in the middle of adding the last touches to the tree when Judy and Lucas arrived with their families tagging behind. After kisses were given and the grandchildren hugged, Judy said, "Merry Christmas, mom and dad! Great job on the Christmas decorations and lights, you guys."

"So what's new ?" Lucas asked with a smile on his face.

They spoke for a while about Christmas and before they knew it, out came the story about their neglect to buy the lottery tickets the night before. Judy and Lucas were as shocked as their parents when they heard the devastating news.

"That's all we can do about it," Jeff stated. "Your mom and I agreed that its over and done with and we can talk about it all we want, but it will never change things. So we decided to not speak about it ever again. Now, let's forget it and enjoy Christmas."

A few minutes later, they all sat in the living room and passed out presents. Several years ago they had started a tradition of giving each other a gift on Christmas Eve and the tradition had continued every year since. Each person passed around their gifts to one another when Lucas said to his parents, "Since you guys have been such great parents to us over the years, Judy and I decided to give you guys that vacation that you always wanted to Jamaica this year. So, here you go, mom and dad, look inside and you'll see this vacation is everything that you have always wanted."

Jeff took the two tickets to Jamaica from Lucas and tears came to his eyes. He flipped open the folder and the first thing that he saw was the lottery tickets that he and Tina had forgotten to buy the night before! He couldn't believe what he was seeing before him. He was speechless. Tina took the tickets from his hand and noticed the lottery tickets sticking out from the folder and, in shock, exclaimed, "How did this happen?"

Lucas responded, "Well, mom and dad, I came by to see you yesterday and when I noticed mom was gone and you fast asleep in your favorite chair, I took the lottery numbers and picked them up at the store. I just figured that you guys forgot and I would make it another small Christmas gift for you. Little did I know that you had won until I checked the numbers this evening. Then Judy and I decided to pull this little prank on you for all the times you have done the same to us." He paused and said with a sly grin, "Merry Christmas. Hope this makes for a happy one for you both."

Both Jeff and Tina jumped to their feet and grabbed both Judy and Lucas exuberantly, showering them with hugs and kisses.

"You guys are great kids. Did I ever tell you, Lucas, that you are my favorite son and you, Judy, my favorite daughter?" Jeff teased amid much shouting of joy.

"That you did, dad, seeing as we are your only son and daughter," Lucas laughed.

- RJH

(My mom, Maggie, who makes the best bread.)

MAGGIE'S BREAD
(By Lisa J. Ivany)

The suffusion of tantalizing smells penetrates homes during Christmas and evokes pleasurable sensations in many people. For some, it's the aroma of turkey, cooking in the oven, or the fresh pine-scented needles from the tree, or even a sweetly glazed ham on the table. However, for me, there is no better fragrance this season than the smell of mom's homemade bread, fresh from the oven. I have yet to build an immunity to this pungent aroma and even though baking bread is a weekly ritual for my mother, at Christmas it still gets top billing in the scent category.

Growing up in Gander, my favorite place in the house was the kitchen as this was the focal point of activity. Every Saturday morning, resplendent in apron and bandana, mom would tirelessly knead dough over and over until the texture was to her satisfaction. While it was rising, her hands were never idle. On the contrary; she would have cakes, cookies, pies, or some other sweet concoction made and baked by the time the dough had risen. I'd watch through fascinated eyes as she lopped off chunks of dough, rolled them in little logs, and placed three of these in each pan, looking like little baby's butts with an extra cheek. This little analogy often caused me to giggle.

With the delicious scent of bread wafting throughout the house, it wasn't long before I was joined by my siblings to await the cutting of the first loaf. On retrieving the loaves from the oven, mom would spread a layer of butter over the tops of each golden mound, making them shiny and even more desirable. Once cut, we would lather molasses and butter atop the thick slices and smack our lips as the sticky topping oozed down our chins, to be licked pleasurably away as we savored every morsel. This was the Utopia of tastebuds and we'd challenge anyone who spoke to the contrary.

As much as we enjoyed mom's bread, she would end up giving most of it away as she had the heart of a saint and there were always willing recipients in the form of relatives, friends, and neighbours. My father always joked that if mom made seven loaves of bread, she would give away eight.

Christmastime has always been a busy time for mom, accelerating to overdrive mode. Upon entering her kitchen, one's senses would immediately be assailed by the unmistakable scent of holiday baking from bread to vanilla to cinnamon. Displayed along two lengths of counter top there would be a cornucopia of mouth-watering delights in the form of cookies, squares, fruit-cakes, and bread. Not only white bread, but at Christmas, she would have several loaves of raisin bread, for it was a Newfoundland tradition for many people to eat fish and raisin bread on Christmas Eve. Of course, like everything else she made, her raisin bread always found its way into other homes.

I remember one time when I was a teenager, a few days before Christmas, and mom had toiled all day, baking for other people and really looked tired. I asked her, "Mom, why do you work so hard baking for other people when you never seem to get anything in return?"

She looked at me quizzically and said, "Lisa, I don't do it for any reward. I do it because I enjoy it and it makes people happy."

"But mom," I replied. "You work so hard and sometimes people don't even seem to appreciate the effort you put into it. I don't understand why you do it."

"Someday I'm sure you'll understand and maybe follow in my footsteps."

"I don't think so," I defiantly rebuked.

She chuckled and responded, "I said the same thing to your grandmother when I was about your age. You might as well face it, this is something that's passed down through the generations. It's in our blood. You'll see when the time comes."

The years passed and mom continued her tradition of giving, not only at Christmas, but all through the year as well. At times, I thought it was well worth her effort when she gave to people who did nice things for her and really seemed to appreciate her efforts. For instance, my boss, Dr. Joe Tumilty, an orthopaedic surgeon, was readily available to provide assistance whenever mom needed his services over the years with her troublesome shoulder. Therefore, I felt any baking she did for him was well deserved.

The reputation of mom's wonderful bread preceded her from the older generations, down to the younger. This was enforced one Christmas Eve when I visited Joe, his wife Sue, and their two little girls. Sue told me how much they had enjoyed the loaf of bread mom had given them the previous day, especially their two girls, Alex and Kate, who ate every crumb. The next morning when asked if they wanted toast for breakfast, Kate asked if it was *Maggie's bread*. Her mother said it was all gone, to which Kate turned up her nose, and declined the offer. Up to this point the girls had never met my mother, yet knew the difference between *her* bread and what was bought at the store, and definitely preferred the former.

This past Christmas Eve when I was preparing some tins of baked treats for my friends and neighbors, mom walked in and said, "Hi dear. What are you doing?"

I responded, "Just putting together some goodies for friends."

"Are you doing a cookie exchange or is this part of their Christmas gifts?"

"Actually neither," I replied. "This is just a little something extra I wanted to give them to spread around a little holiday cheer. I enjoy doing it." Indeed, I seemed to have a warm glow inside as I filled the holiday tins with an array of toffee squares, chewy snowballs, chocolate drops, and pecan tarts, to name a few. I was thinking how wonderful it was going to be when my friends received their cans of treats.

She laughed and said, "You are your mother's daughter alright. I'm so glad to see you following in my footsteps."

Up to that point I hadn't realized what a valuable lesson I had learned from my mother. By watching her over the years, giving away hundreds of loaves of bread and thousands of baked treats, I finally understood that giving something without the expectation of a reward was the actual reward itself. It may be perceived by others as though you are giving them a gift, but the feeling you get inside is actually the greatest gift of all.

I may never be able to replicate *Maggie's bread*, but I will use her key ingredient in whatever I set out to do - a large dash of love.

This Christmas, as I watch my mother handing

out her baked treasures, I smile, for I know the holiday spirit is radiating within her heart in all its glory. How do I know this? Because I have the same feeling as my trays of cookies are being escorted to various homes. The last recipient of one of my trays paid me the nicest compliment I could ever receive; she told me I was just like my mother.

- LJI

IN THE HEAT OF THE MOMENT
(By Robert J. Hunt)

All Paul Ryan could remember was the profuse burning sensation he felt as flames engulfed him and the weight of the protected package that was folded in his arms. The heat and weight alone almost caused him to give up and rush to his final destination. He dropped low to the floor as the downdraft and smoke encircled him overhead. He felt as if he were another person in his own body trying to get out. His breathing apparatus started to fog up with smoke as he progressed towards the light ahead at the end of the darkened semi-lit hall-way. Twenty, or maybe thirty feet to go and he would be out. Every step felt as if his legs and fire-protected suit weighed 250 pounds and stuck on his 5' 10", 190 pound frame. He checked his watch and made a final dash for freedom and outside into the fresh air. The door ... concentrate on the door, he thought as he slowly fought tears and dizziness. He emerged at the hallway's end and burst out into the warm, sunny day. Though it was the 20th of December, it was over 16C.

"You did it, Paul! You did it!" his fellow fire-fighting buddy, Art Long, shouted in his ear. "You made it, you hero."

As he emerged from the smoking building, a round of applause greeted him from his fellow competitors who had gathered for the 10th annual Corner Brook Firefighters Challenge. Paul dropped his 25 pound "teddy bear" package, ripped off his mask, and sucked in the golden air. A large group of firefighters circled around him and began showering him with handshakes as his time was posted on the area clock.

"A new record of 7 minutes 22 seconds," his colleagues shouted and clapped. "You must have a sixth sense to get through that maze in record time."

Paul lifted his head in triumph amid shouts and well wishes from firefighters from his Bay Roberts Unit as well as those from other fire stations. He had successfully maneuvered the "Maze," as it was called, and had done so in record time, cutting over 50 seconds off the best time! He was proud of his achievements as a firefighter and his ratio to saving lives in a real fire was twice as high as any of his friends in the unit.

Art gazed over at Paul and smiled. "Is there anything you can't do, hero?" he joked.

Paul nodded yes and glanced down at Art's artificial leg. He remembered how he had pulled Art from a burning paint building three years earlier. They had saved two people from burning to death and had entered to save a third when a wall collapsed, trapping Art underneath. Paul frantically got the third person out of the building and then rushed back in to save his friend. Managing to free him was easier than he thought, but the fire and fallen wall had done their damage. In the process of freeing Art, Paul had to literally tear his leg from underneath the wall's weight. The end result, though he saved Art's life, was that his leg had to be amputated from the knee down. Paul had always blamed himself for that although Art knew he had saved his life.

"Better get cleaned up, Hero, and out of that monkey suit. We have to get a good night's sleep for our trip back to Bay Roberts in the morning," Art stated.

Paul smiled at his friend. Art had such a robust personality and loved kidding him. He knew how much he appreciated saving him from the warehouse fire, but Paul always regretted not getting to him early enough to save his leg. But that was Art and he had kept Paul's spirits high for years concerning his accident and always called him his "Hero." Art was always "Mr. Positive," Paul thought.

After the awards were handed out and handshakes and congratulations were showered on all, Paul and Art packed up their belongings, said goodbye to their buddies, and started their long eight hour drive back to Bay Roberts.

Driving along the Trans Canada Highway, they both alleviated the boredom by telling jokes about friends, family, and their jobs and talked of their route to becoming firefighters, even the fact that due to his leg amputation Art now worked behind a desk instead of running into burning buildings. However, this never seemed to bother Art - he felt lucky just to be alive. So engrossed in their laughing and joking, they were halfway there before they knew it.

"Gander is only another few miles, Art," Paul stated. "You're almost as good a driver as I am."

Art leaned towards his friend and playfully responded, "What do you mean as good...."

As soon as the words left his mouth, Paul shouted to his friend, "Watch out!"

Art glanced quickly from the corner of his eye to catch a glimpse of a gigantic moose darting across the firefighters' truck from the trees. Twisting the wheel to the right, they braced themselves for the impact. In a matter of seconds the world stood still. The vehicle zoomed by the rear of the animal, down an embankment, and struck a clump of tress. It continued to roll, flipping over and over for 100 feet or so, tearing up rock, dirt, and soil as its speed started to decrease. After several revolutions, it stopped and landed on its roof.

Art felt as if he wanted to throw up. His head felt as though something had hit it with a hammer. For several seconds he was dazed. It took him time to readjust to what had happened in the last few moments. Getting his bearings, he realized what had transpired and looked around for Paul. Frantically, he checked himself for injury and realized his left arm was bleeding and there was blood between his fingers. No matter, Paul was his first concern.

"Paul! Where are you buddy?" No answer.

He became frantic. Calm down and check out the situation, he thought. He looked around the cab again. There was still no sign of Paul. Then he heard it ... a light gasping sound, just barely audible.

"Art ... help me, I'm over here."

Art looked around. Uncomfortable and slanted upside down, Art turned his torso slightly and looked in the direction of the voice. Barely visible was part of Paul's sweater. He started to slide towards Paul. At once, the truck creaked and moved to one side, shifting precariously. "Art, don't move! We're on the edge of a deep ravine and any sudden jarring could topple us."

Art knew the truck was after flipping over and was balanced on the edge of a cliff. From what he could gather, Paul was holding on for dear life, dangling high above the ravine. He assessed the situation and looked to his left. He noticed a large tree trunk about six feet from his position. Slowly he reached behind the back seat and secured a 100 foot firefighters' safety rope that was already looped for these kinds of situations. In a sharp voice he hollered, "Paul, hold on! I'm going to try and hook this rope around a tree trunk a few feet away and pull you to safety. Please don't move for a few seconds. I'm going to get you out of this, my friend."

He made a loop knot and proceeded to loop it around the tree. After several tries, it finally secured itself and Art tugged tightly to hold it in place. He inched himself towards Paul and the door that was torn off on impact. With the sudden movement, the truck's cab tilted a few inches on the ledge that held it. Only a few feet separated him from Paul. Art moved back to his original position by the driver's door and took a few deep breaths.

"Paul, listen to me," he said. "I can't go towards you as the truck will topple off this cliff, but I have an idea. I'm going to secure this rope to a tree trunk next to me and then throw you the end. Wrap it around yourself as best you can and I'll pull you towards me, okay?"

"Art, I'm hanging on by a thread here. You can't take the chance of my weight pulling you down. I want you to pull yourself free of this mess and let me go. The truck's ready to go any second and I don't want you to go over with me to the bottom of this canyon. Please, Art, listen to me," he pleaded.

Art looked towards the passenger side of the truck and spoke softly, "Listen to me, Paul. What you said is not an option. Either both of us make it or both of us go over. End of discussion. I remember how you came back for me in that paint warehouse fire years ago and saved my life. I also know that you have been blaming yourself for me losing my leg when you shouldn't have. Now it's my turn, Hero. Both of us are getting out of this alive or I go over with you. Do you understand?"

"Okay, partner, let's do it," he answered. "When you tug, tug hard. I think my right arm is broken so I won't be much help to you so you'll have to bear practically all my weight."

Art made another loop and threw it towards the door. Paul had to slip the rope around him with his broken arm. It was with slow movement and considerable pain that he finally secured himself. In a weak voice, he said, "Okay, I'm secure and ready when you are. But one thing, Art, if you see that you can't make it with my weight, I want you to promise to let me go and save yourself. Right?"

Art looked towards the door and smiled. "Sorry, buddy, I can't hear you. It must be the impact and confusion. As I said, two of us or neither of us. Get ready."

Art strained with all his might. His body ached and his arms started to cramp. Slowly, Paul started to appear in the door's opening. He pulled slower and slower as the truck started to move. Art could feel the ground start to give way beneath them. The cab inched toward its final destination. Art made a desperate grab for Paul's shirt. After securing it, he pulled hard. The rope around the tree trunk became taut as both were hauled towards the opening and freedom a few feet from the cliff's edge. They both landed on the soft earth. Art looked towards the space where the truck was and heard the crash and bang as it continued its descent down the ravine.

After a few minutes of catching their breath, Art assessed how lucky they were not to be a part of the flaming truck lying 200 feet below them.

"We made it, Art. We made it!" Paul exclaimed. He looked his friend in the eye, winked, and said, "Now you're the Hero."

"Yeah, I am aren't I," he chuckled in high spirits.

The two survivors lay side-by-side as they listened to a blaring siren, signaling the approach of an ambulance and their imminent rescue. Realizing they had cheated death once again, the two friends laughed uncontrollably. They were still shaking with mirth as they were carried on stretcher boards up the embankment to the highway.

After being settled away in the back of the ambulance, Paul looked over at his friend and said, "Merry Christmas, Hero."

Art responded, "Merry Christmas, Hero."

- RJH

Christmas Eve Journey

She looks through the window
On this Christmas Eve night
To the blizzard that's raging
Painting everything white

Her husband had left
A few hours before
And since he's been gone
She's been pacing the floor

The storm came on quickly
A while after he'd gone
She prays for his safety
And hopes nothing goes wrong

He packed for his journey
Then got on his way
Kissed his sweet wife goodbye
As he boarded his sleigh

He pops down through chimneys
With a red velvet sack
To bring presents to children
Before heading back

She hears the jingle of bells
As the reindeer hit ground
Mrs. Claus is relieved
For Santa's back safe and sound

Lisa J. Ivany

A HELPING HAND
(By Lisa J. Ivany)

Trudy Nelson stirred her tea in the corner table of the cafeteria, enjoying the temporary silence. She had finished typing the consults for Dr. Frampton ahead of schedule and went on her break early, arriving before anyone else.

She started her secretarial position at the James Paton Memorial Hospital in Gander after just turning 18. She had moved to the town from Eastport and had only planned on staying until she saved enough money to move to the Mainland. However, a local night club owner swept her off her feet and she changed her mind about leaving. That was 20 years ago and she never regretted her decision to stay in the beautiful town or of marrying Barry.

Trudy absentmindedly toyed with her long brunette curls, hanging just below her shoulders. Big sapphire eyes creased in contemplation below thin furrowed brows. Under a short pert nose, her bronze-tinted lips were contorted in a slight grimace. In her mind, she rehashed her dilemma once again. Her staff Christmas party and Barry's were both next Saturday night and they could not reach an agreement on which one to attend. On the one hand, Barry had already given his staff the night off to attend the party and sent out public notices that the club would be closed. On the other hand, Trudy's last chance to socialize with Beth would be at the hospital party. Beth and Trudy had become close friends after sharing an office for 15 years, but Beth had just retired and was moving to Cartwright, Labrador in a few days with her new husband.

"Did you hear the news?" a shrill voice exclaimed, intruding upon Trudy's thoughts.

"What news?"

Joan Seaward plumped her tall hefty frame in the seat across from Trudy and continued, "Sandie and Bill Prescott split up over the weekend."

Joan's panther-like eyes gleamed as she relayed her juicy tale. Although her workload as a Management Director kept her busy, she always found time to spread fresh rumors. Her wavy shoulder length black hair bounced against her rounded face as she twisted her head to see if anyone else had heard her news. By this time, the cafeteria was filling up as the morning coffee break had started.

"Good morning, ladies," Phyllis Hayley stated in her usual flat monotone, seating herself at the table.

Trudy often wondered why there were people on earth like Phyllis who had a permanently dismal attitude. She might have passed as attractive if not for the perpetual frown etched across her face. Her silky red hair flowed loosely to her shoulders in large waves, encompassing a pale oval face. A thin sprinkling of pale freckles lightly touched her thin nose and cheeks, barely perceptible to the naked eye.

Joan asked Phyllis, "Did you hear that Sandie and Bill Prescott split up?"

"No, but it's not surprising," Phyllis responded.

"He's been fooling around on her for years."

"Well apparently Sandie dropped by his office on Saturday and caught him with the cleaning lady," Joan remarked. "And believe me, she wasn't cleaning his office." Her lips smirked and her eyebrows raised in excitement on imparting this last tidbit, reinforcing the reason she was known as the hospital gossip.

Trudy didn't normally sit with the *dreadful duo*, however, when Joan was spreading a fresh rumor, she slithered from one table to another, telling everyone in her path. Phyllis followed her around like a lost puppy.

"Have you seen the notice about the EFAP Christmas hampers?" Trudy asked, trying to steer the topic of conversation in a different direction.

"Yeah," Phyllis replied. "What does EFAP stand for anyway?"

"It's for Employee and Family Assistance Program. Hospital employees donate money to the EFAP Committee who, in turn, buy hampers for staff members who need a helping hand at Christmas," answered Trudy.

Joan piped in, "I know you're on the EFAP Committee, Trudy, but I think it's all a hoax. If someone is getting a pay cheque, they don't need handouts from the rest of us."

"You're not getting the point," Trudy defended. "These hampers are only given to staff who really need them."

"Yeah, well who would qualify?"

"Sometimes there are single mothers, raising a family without spousal support," Trudy responded. "We have also had medically ill staff members who have racked up quite a large debt traveling to St. John's or even out of the province for treatment. There have also been employees who have left their marriages with vir-tually the clothes on their backs. These are just a few examples, but there many reasons people end up in financial distress."

A gleam brightened Joan's eyes as she asked, "Do you know who will be getting the hampers this year?"

Trudy replied, "All names remain confidential."

Disgruntled at not receiving this desired information to pass around as the latest rumor, Joan said, "Well, I'm not donating if I don't know where my money is going."

"Then don't," Trudy replied. "It's your choice if you want to lend a helping hand."

Weary of the conversation, Trudy left the cafeteria. Before she made it through the door, she heard Joan relaying her latest gossip about the Prescotts to staff at the next table. Rolling her eyes and shaking her head, she felt sorry for Joan's latest captive audience.

When Trudy returned to her office, there was a yellow post-it note on her computer monitor from Beth. She had dropped in to pick up her tickets to the Christmas party and left a reminder for Trudy to do the same because the deadline was Thursday. She moaned audibly, wondering how she would tell her friend she most probably would not be joining her. With the deadline just three days away, she would have to make a decision soon. She was still hoping to find a way to attend.

Although a part of Trudy resented Barry for preventing her from being with Beth for her last party in Gander, she understood his point as well. He was hosting the dinner and dance for his employees and the date had been set and notices sent out weeks ago when they were told the hospital party was the weekend before. However, due to an error in reservations, the hospital party was later switched to the same night as Barry's party. All his employees had the night off and were looking forward to attending the party. Barry needed to be there because he and Trudy were doing all the cooking so that the kitchen staff could relax and enjoy themselves as well. It was an annual tradition which Barry did not want to break.

At coffee break the next morning, Trudy sat at a table with many of her co-workers and was surprised to see Phyllis get in the lineup for tea by herself. It was very rare to not see her tagging along behind Joan.

Once through the queue, Phyllis looked around for a place to sit and settled in the empty chair next to Trudy.

"Morning," Phyllis mumbled flatly. Before anyone could respond, she continued, "I guess you've all heard about Joan and Carson."

The murmuring at the table lessened as the different conversations lulled to hear what bit of news Phyllis was talking about. Someone piped up, "No, what news?"

"Apparently Carson kicked Joan out on the street last night. When she got home from work yesterday, he had her bags packed on the step and the locks changed."

Trudy was not interested in listening to this gossip, however, Freda, who was sitting next to her, felt differently. Freda exclaimed, "Why? Did he catch her fooling around with someone?"

"No. Apparently Joan had relayed some information to Carson's boss which he didn't like," Phyllis responded. "She told him the rumor about the Prescotts, not knowing that Carson's boss was Sandie Prescott's father. When Carson found out, he flipped! He told her he was sick of listening to her constant gossiping and told her not to come back."

Freda asked, "Where is she now?"

"Birchview Apartments," Phyllis replied. "She was lucky enough to find a vacancy right away. However, she had to pay first and last month's rent which practically took all her money. She's not doing very well financially."

Trudy interjected, "Phyllis, I don't understand why you're spreading this information around about Joan. I thought she was your friend?"

"She is, but it's just as well for me to spread it around. If not, someone else will anyway."

"That's a great attitude," Trudy sarcastically retorted. "I see Joan has trained you well."

At this uncharacteristic bluntness, Trudy left the table to the sound of startled gasps from her co-workers.

Although Joan was certainly not on Trudy's list of favorite people, she empathized with her situation. She thought it was hard enough being alone after many years of marriage, but to be thrown out of your home this close to Christmas must be devastating. Obviously, Joan's gossiping got her into this mess, but you would have to be pretty insensitive not to feel sorry for her, Trudy thought.

Later that evening, Trudy walked with trepidation down the corridor of Birchview Apartments, looking for Apartment 106. She was uneasy about the reception she would get from Joan, especially when she told her the reason for her visit. There was certainly no difficulty getting the number of Joan's apartment through the grapevine. Trudy would have preferred calling her, but she knew Joan did not yet have her new phone hooked up.

She rapped loudly on the door and heard a slow shuffling gait, however, the door did not open. She knocked again, more loudly this time and called out, "Joan, I know you're in there. Please let me in."

Trudy waited a few moments and then heard the latch being unlocked. The door swung in slowly, to reveal a haggard-looking woman with bloodshot eyes, a red blotchy nose, disheveled clothes, and hair sticking out in uneven tufts. This was hardly the impeccably groomed and confident woman Trudy knew from work.

"What do you want?" Joan snapped.

"If you let me in, I'll tell you."

Joan stepped back to allow Trudy entrance into her new place. She added, "I'd offer you a seat, but as you can see, I don't have any furniture yet."

Indeed, Trudy thought as she gazed around the bare apartment, this was certainly a major step down from the beautiful manor Joan had in the new area of town. The absence of furniture and any Christmas decorations created quite a dismal scene.

"How are you doing?" Trudy asked.

"How do you think?" Joan snarled. "Now, why are you here?"

"Well, I've heard you're going through a rough time right now and I'd like permission to submit your name for a Christmas hamper?"

"Do I look like a charity case to you?"

"Of course not. However, everyone needs a helping hand from time-to-time and I thought you might need one now." Trudy coaxed, "Please accept the offer in the good faith that it's extended."

"No thanks. I'd never be able to raise my head at work again if people knew I had received a hamper."

"No one will know. As I told you before, it's kept confidential."

With reluctance, Joan asked, "Are you positive that absolutely no one outside the EFAP Committee will know?"

"I guarantee you, it's totally confidential."

"Well, I guess I'd be a fool not to accept," she relented.

On Saturday, the 20th of December, while waltzing to the seasonal carol, *Pretty Paper*, Trudy thanked

Barry once again for his compromise. They had dinner with his employees and stayed for a few dances, then left to join Beth and her husband at the hospital party. Everyone was in high spirits although Trudy was a little sad, knowing she would not see Beth after tonight for a long time.

When Barry led Trudy from the dance floor, she felt a tap on her shoulder. She turned to find Joan and Carson hand-in-hand.

"Trudy, may I have a word with you in private?" Joan asked.

"Of course. The corridor is empty if you'd like to go out there."

The two ladies excused themselves from their spouses and went to a secluded corner at the end of the hallway.

Joan began, "Last night Carson agreed to give our marriage another chance and I'm back home now. However, I wanted to thank you for the hamper. It really helped me out of a rough spot and I don't know how I would have made it through without it."

"There is no need to thank me. The EFAP Committee is there to help any staff member when needed. I'm glad we could help you out."

Joan extracted a slip of paper from her jacket pocket and handed it to Trudy. She said, "Now that I'm in a better financial situation, I'd like to give this donation to use for your hampers next year."

Trudy accepted the cheque and was amazed at the amount. She said, "This is far too generous, Joan. There is no need to donate such a large amount."

"Please accept this in the good faith that it's given. I've come to learn how important these hampers are to the staff members who truly need a helping hand."

A voice interrupted, "Hi ladies."

They turned to see Freda practically sprinting down the corridor with a greasy grin on her face. She exclaimed, "Have you heard the latest news about Ken and Valerie Rowsell?"

"No," Joan replied, "and I don't want to either."

Freda watched in open-mouthed amazement as Joan and Trudy returned to the dance without listening to her latest news.

- LJI

(Carmel Hunt as a young woman.)

CHRISTMAS HEARTBEAT
(By Robert J. Hunt)

The year was 1957. I was eight years old and living in St. John's, Newfoundland. I remember thinking that this would probably be her last Christmas. She had suffered for a long time with a rheumatic heart and the years of taking medication were starting to catch up with her. I can see her now, only 39 years of age, but suffering from a heart condition since she was 24. She had moved in a slow motion state since that time, just one small step after another. Her head movements and walking pattern were similar to a turtle in a race with ... well, a hare, but this time the turtle could not win.

My visions of her when I was a young man were the same as all young men at eight years of age - she was my mom and she would live forever. I remember the nights when I would go to bed and I could hear her footsteps coming up the stairway of our three-storey house. It would take her at least 20 minutes to climb those stairs, but she always did to say goodnight to me and my brothers.

I will always remember that I was her special son, or at least that's what she always said to me and it didn't matter if she said the same thing to my four other brothers or not. The words she said were, for me, very special at that time in a young child's life. She was my mom and no one else's!

It all started one Christmas night when she made that special trek upstairs to say her regular goodnight to my brothers and me. Her breathing was unusually heavy and labored. After saying goodnight to them, she came to my bed and kissed me on the cheek. I always remember how her heart used to beat as she held me close to her. I recall thinking how could she have a bad heart when it is beating so perfectly. Surely she couldn't be sick - the doctors were wrong about my mom! That night she held me extra tight as I listened to her heartbeat. She whispered to me, I guess, so my brothers would not hear.

"Hi, my little prince. Listen to my heart. It beats for you and your brothers and it will even when I am no longer here. It will always say when you hear it, that I love all of you very much. Listen to it now and always remember." She gave me a big hug and held me to her breast.

"Boom, boom, boom ... I love you, I love you," it said.

Every night after that, as I was held close by my mother, nine years before she died, I used to tell her that she didn't have to tell me she loved me, that I could hear it in her heartbeat. I was her special prince and she and I would live forever!

Mom passed away ten years later, in July of 1967, after a heart transplant failed to help her. I was seventeen years old when she died and I still remember thinking that I couldn't hear her heartbeat because she was two thousand miles away in Toronto. I was only eight on that Christmas night when she told me to listen to her heartbeat and for nine more beautiful years she didn't have to tell me she loved me, for her heartbeat always told me so. Her last thoughts and her last words were for her boys, for she apparently told the nurse at her bedside:

"Tell my little princes I love them ... and heart-beat ..." That is all she said. To this day, when I hear a heartbeat, those words of so long ago always come to mind and I now recall that Christmas of 1967 with such fond memories and also the beautiful words of that wonderful woman with the heavenly heartbeat.

- RJH

A WINNING SPIRIT
(By Lisa J. Ivany)

It's neck and neck around the bend as Trixie and Newton's Beauty keep pace! the announcer spewed. *Now Finnigan's Bluff pulls into third position just barely ahead of Thunderbolt with mere inches separating them from Sprinter and Gold Rush. Lagging behind, it seems Flash Filly will have a hard time regaining lost time and staying firm in last place once again is Shetty. It seems this old horse has a permanent position at the rear here at the Calgary Track.*

Gus Pritchett's breath held as he watched Trixie maintaining her first place position, going into the home stretch. He had placed quite a sizable bet on Trixie at twenty to one odds and was saying a silent prayer that she would win.

Finally the announcer said, *The winner of the final race of the day is Trixie!*

"Yes-s-s-s!" Gus exclaimed with his deep throaty brogue. A few heads turned as this hefty, broad-shouldered man with thick curly black hair and beard jumped up and down in his enthusiasm. He was like a big overgrown teddy bear when he got excited and one of the reasons he was the favorite uncle of his three charges. When he won a trip for four to Alberta on a ticket he purchased back home in Port au Choix, Newfoundland, he automatically knew whom he would take with him.

With the Christmas season so near, Gus' brother and his wife were a little reluctant to let their children go, however, they relented when they saw how much it meant to them.

"Can we leave now?" Tony asked.

Gus looked down at his14 year old nephew and said, "We can go anywhere you want, my boy, as soon as I collect my winnings and find your sisters. Now, where have they gone?"

"The last time I saw them, Karly was trying to tear Leah away from the stalls again. She sure loves those horses."

After pocketing his windfall, Gus scanned the accumulation of patrons for two auburn ponytails. He knew he'd have difficulty locating Leah with her short stature, in keeping with her eight years, however, Karly would be a little easier to spot with her tall lean frame similar to that of her twin brother, Tony. He scanned the crowd and went row by row searching for his nieces, to no avail.

With his nephew in tow, Gus headed for the stalls. Before he reached the aisle of wooden cubicles housing the horses, he heard Leah's shrieks. The Pritchett men raced simultaneously towards the sound of her agonized wailing, fearing the worst.

"What's wrong?" Tony asked his little sister, arriving on the scene first.

Tears poured from her big blue eyes as she stared woefully into the stall named "Shetty." Karly's matching eyes were also moisture-laden as she stared in the same direction with an arm around her little sister's shoulders. Her efforts to divert Leah's attention from the ruckus in the stall were futile.

Whipping sounds followed by painful whinnies came from behind the wooden gate. From inside the stall, a man's angered voice screamed, "You good for nothing bag of bones! I should have sent you off to the slaughter house years ago and had you packaged into steaks." He raised the whip again and brought it sharply down upon the hindquarters of the horse who lay whimpering. "I can't believe I've wasted so much time and effort on a horse who has never won a single race!"

The furious man raised the lash above his head again, but before it landed on the horse, his arm was seized in a vice-like grip. Startled, he looked up into the fearsome eyes of Gus Pritchett and knew he had met his match.

"Hey, what do you want?" the man croaked.

"I want you to pretend to be that horse and I'll pretend to be you," Gus replied menacingly as he yanked the weapon out of the scrawny man's hand.

Fearing a lashing similar to the one he had just bestowed on the helpless animal, he slowly backed away from Gus until he was brought up solid by the back corner of the stall. His beady grey eyes darted in all directions for a route of escape, however, Gus Pritchett encompassed all perimeters. The man's legs were quite visibly shaking and beads of sweat had quickly formed above his brows.

Slowly, Gus gathered in the whip, forming loops, then released them to the ground while still clasping the handle. He then flicked it so that it lightly touched the stall's floor, then once again, a little higher this time, and with a harder jolt.

As he toyed with the lash, getting higher and harder each time, Gus's gaze never wavered from his foe's face. Terror etched the man's countenance, to the point where he finally pleaded, "Please don't hurt me, mister. I promise I won't do it again, but please let me walk out of here unharmed."

"That's not good enough," Gus snarled. "As

soon as I leave, I'm sure you'll be back torturing this beautiful animal again. So, I think I will have to let you know how these lashes feel first hand."

"No, I swear, I will not hurt Shetty again. In fact, you can have him free of charge if you want him. I have no more use for him."

Leah, overhearing this news, quickly scurried into the stall and asked, "Uncle Gus, can we really take him home with us? Can we ... oh please!"

He bent down over the beaten horse, sizing up its injuries, and realized the horse would probably not make it through the night due to the extent of the damage inflicted. Shetty's breath was shallow and from the looks of things, he had lost a lot of blood. His once shiny brown coat was now matted with several lines of coagulated blood while other fresh ones still oozed. However, when Gus looked into Leah's hopeful and concerned eyes, he didn't have the heart to mention the horse's prognosis.

He hadn't noticed the man slither away while he was ministering to the animal, but he was now nowhere in sight. It was just as well because the anger inside Gus at the abuse caused by the nasty weasel of a man probably would have caused him to do something he would have regretted later ... or probably not.

"Well, Leah, you know it's only another week and we have to fly back home to Newfoundland. How are we going to get a horse on a plane?"

"Why don't we rent a truck and a horse trailer and drive," suggested Karly. "I heard that Trixie won the race so you probably won enough to cover it."

"Yeah," Tony piped in, joining in his sister's crusade to save Shetty. "You were a big winner today and why not put your money to good use."

Leah looked up again and pleaded, "Please, Uncle Gus."

"Okay, okay. I can't very well fight three of you," he relented. "If he makes it through the night, I'll make arrangements to take him back to Newfoundland with us. However, we will have to cut our trip short to give us enough time to drive across the country and be home in time for Christmas or your mother will never forgive me."

Gus was almost toppled over by the enthusiastic hugs from three pairs of arms embracing him at the same time.

The next morning, the veterinarian informed Gus that Shetty had made it through the night although he was not out of the woods yet. Due to the severity of the injuries sustained, his chances for survival were 50/50 at best. Being a betting man, Gus did not like those odds at all, but in order to make it home for Christmas, he would have to start the long drive home now. He was taking a risk, but decided to have the horse transported to the trailer he had rented, being pulled by a large navy van.

Shetty's strength seemed to weaken over the ensuing few days as he lay on the floor of the trailer in a semi-comatose condition. Valuable travel time was lost as the four occupants of the van periodically stopped and ministered to the ailing animal's wounds and ensured he was kept warm. Another hindrance was from Mother Nature when a two-day blizzard kept them off the Trans Canada Highway in Manitoba.

The ferry ride from Nova Scotia to Newfoundland was a rough passage as they were getting the tail end of the blizzard. The lapping waves loomed large and fierce, tossing the boat unsteadily from side-to-side. All passengers were advised to stay in their berths until further notice for their own safety, so the Pritchett family was not able to check on Shetty below. They feared she would not make it through the night.

Early the next morning, on the 21st of December, the sun was shining and the sapphire waves lay calm upon the water, in contrast to the previous night.

In trepidation, Gus opened the back of the trailer and to his astonishment, Shetty was standing for the first time since the journey started. She gratefully accepted the apple extended to her from Leah's small hand and sniffed the air as if trying to get her bearings. She snorted once and shook her head with a strength and interest she had not shown since her new owners took possession of her.

The drive from Port-aux-Basques to Corner Brook went uneventfully and the travelers enjoyed the scenic snow-covered trees and mountains. The early morning sun bathed the snow in its radiance, causing millions of snow crystals to twinkle like rhinestones. Clear blue sky stretched endlessly overhead, that is, until they were a few miles outside of Pasadena. Then the idyllic Christmas card scenery changed drastically. Dark voluminous clouds studded the sky and the sun had completely disappeared. Within minutes visibility was virtually nil as the van was peppered with sweeping blankets of snow.

Gus turned on the radio and heard the warning for all travelers on the West Coast that most of the highway was snow-covered and slippery. There was a blizzard warning for the Northern Peninsula and the snow plows had been called off the roads.

"I guess we'll have to stay overnight in Pasadena," Gus stated to the kids. "There's no way we'll make it to Port au Choix today."

"There, up ahead," Tony said, pointing to a sign. "Mintville Cabins. That's where I stayed with my soccer team last year when we came out here for a tournament. The cabins are new and they have a barn out back we can put Shetty in."

"Sounds good to me," Gus replied.

"But it's almost Christmas," Leah moaned. "We have to get home to mommy and daddy."

"I'll give them a call so they don't worry," Gus responded. "When the weather clears off, we'll get going, little one. We'll be home in time for Christmas."

Leah seemed satisfied with her uncle's reassurance although Gus, himself, was not so sure. From listening to the radio, it seemed they were in for a couple of days of bad weather and he knew how treacherous the Northern Peninsula could be in such harsh winter conditions.

Two days later, the stranded travelers were still detained at the cabins, but the blizzard had abated and they decided to continue their journey to make it home for Christmas. The homeward trek northward proved difficult with periodic white-outs, freezing rain, and heavy flurries.

By the time they reached Port Saunders, the road was completely impassable and they could go no farther. The long journey since they had left Calgary, the worry over Shetty's recovery, and the strain of driving in such inclement weather had taken a toll on the weary travelers.

"Well, we have two options," Gus said bleakly. "We can either travel back the way we came and try again tomorrow or we can hike through Old Vinnie's field just up this road and see if the old cabin is still standing and stay there for the night."

"Who's Vinnie?" asked Karly.

"He's an old friend of mine who died a few years back," Gus replied. "We used to spend summers at his cabin when we were boys and Vinnie lived there after he retired. It's been vacant since he passed away and I'm hoping the key's in the same hiding place. There's a small stable there as well to keep Shetty comfortable for the night, or at least I hope it's still there."

"His ghost won't be there, will it?" Leah asked skeptically.

"Of course not," Gus replied.

"Then let's go to the cabin," Leah answered.

As luck would have it, the cabin and stable were intact and the key was in the same place as Gus remembered. They spent a peaceful night, comforted by the warmth of the fire in the grate and the snacks they had the foresight to bring with them from the van.

Christmas Eve morning arrived with blue sky and sunshine, however, due to the heavy snowfall overnight, Gus realized it was too deep for them to make it all the way back to the van on foot. It was at least one mile away, if not more. His brows knit in consternation as he tried to figure out a plan of action for this dilemma. Surely, there must be a way to get the kids home for Christmas morning.

What's that sound? he wondered. He was sure he heard the sound of sleigh bells, but where could it be coming from? He scurried to the door and swung it open. To his surprise, standing before him, draped in Christmas ribbons, bells, and holly was Shetty with a double-seated sleigh attached to her festive harness. Tony sat in the front seat with the reins while the girls were huddled together in the back.

"Merry Christmas, Uncle Gus!" they all cheered in unison.

"Come on, let's go home!" Leah squealed with excitement. "We have to get there before Santa arrives!"

"Wow! I had forgotten all about Vinnie's old sleigh," Gus remarked. "It seems like old Vinnie has come through for us again." He bowed his head for a moment and said a silent prayer of thanks to his old friend and then climbed into the seat next to his nephew.

That evening around the dinner table the kids relayed the adventurous trip home to their parents, one trying to outdo the other. Gus sat back and grinned, knowing he would not have been able to get a word in if he tried. He had been smirking since the afternoon when he drove back in the van with Shetty keeping pace by the side of the road, pulling the kids in the sleigh. The residents of Port au Choix gaped in awe to see the magnificent horse-drawn sleigh enter the community in its festive regalia with bells jingling.

Gus thought it was indeed miraculous that just a few days ago this horse lay near death and now she was sprinting down the lane aglow with the Christmas spirit. She was indeed a winner after all.

- LJI

CHRISTMAS TRIVIA

Mummers In Newfoundland

Don't be surprised to hear a knock at your door between December 26 and January 6, with a voice asking, "Any mummers 'lowed in?!" The act of mummering (also known as jannying) has been a tradition in Newfoundland dating back to the earliest settlers from England and Ireland.

It originally started when people strolled through the streets playing practical jokes on friends and passersby. Mummers would disguise themselves using face paint or covering their heads and stuffing their clothes with pillow cases. Men and women would often disguise their voices and dress as the opposite sex to avoid being identified.

This tradition, was well received in Newfoundland outports and eventually spread to the bigger centers. In recent years, mummering has faded and is not as common. However, with the release of "The Mummer's Song," by Simini in 1982, the mummering tradition came back to life in many places on the Island, especially the outports.

Mummers tend to travel in small groups and once inside your door, tend to kick up their heels for a good old Newfoundland scuff. Mummers play instruments, dance, and share the Christmas spirit with anyone who will open their door. Many enjoy the tradition of syrup or spirits along with some fruit cake and Christmas cookies. Once you have figured out who a particular mummer is, the jig is up and they have to uncover their face.

"Any mummers 'lowed in?!"...

ONE RAINY NIGHT
(By Robert J. Hunt)

The torrid downpour cascaded against the windshield of Colin Pittman's car as he drove home on this half-raining, half-snowy night close to Christmas. The constant battering of wind shook the car as it moved along the road and had Colin gripping the wheel for control as his mind wandered around thoughts of a new company takeover.

Listed as one of Canada's top young corporate executives, he was noted in the Forbes 500 as one of the richest men in Canada and as a "mover and shaker" in the corporate world of business, stocks, and bonds. His power extended even beyond areas he once thought untouchable and he now controlled companies and businesses that he could only dream of years ago.

At age 43, with 30 million a year in earnings, he was wealthy beyond his wildest dreams. In business, he was known as the "Stock Ghost" for the quick way he swept into and took over a failing company that was in financial difficulty. He now controlled or influenced over 60 companies in Newfoundland and personally owned 22 of those and had 500 employees under his command. Ruthless and smart in business, other executives knew better than to try and fight the "Stock Ghost" when it came to a takeover or in Court. When it came to control of a company, it was going to be his!

But with all his wealth and power, there was also a downside. He was once married to the most beautiful lady, in his mind, in St. John's. Rhonda Lake was unique and stole his heart away when he first laid eyes on her at a lawyer's function three years earlier. Five-foot-five with immaculate skin and stunning blue eyes and features, Colin fell immediately in love with her. He was the envy of all his friends to have ended up with "The" Rhonda Lake and was a successful lawyer on his way up the Court ladder of success at Kenny, Long, and Mackay Law Offices. Then he discovered, through a friend, the inside world of stocks and bonds. Within 10 short years he had gone from making $90,000 a year as a lawyer to over $5,000,000 a year! The sky was the limit and he would soon own many companies in Newfoundland. But ultimately, with his 70 hour work weeks, his marriage failed and his wife demanded a divorce. Thankfully, there were no children and the split was a mutual agreement to both parties involved.

Colin became so deep in thought about his business and marriage, he absentmindedly passed his home on Waterford Bridge Road. I'll go to the end of the road and make a U-turn and head back, he thought. The rain still beat relentlessly against his windshield. He started his U-turn at the dead end when halfway around the turn, he caught sight of something moving from the corner of his eye.

In an instant he was staring at a little girl passing very close to the trees at the street's end and she was wearing a white full-length nightgown with beautiful long blonde hair and piercing sea blue eyes that looked directly at him. She looked quickly at him and walked in through the trees.

"What the hell?" Colin said, as he stopped the car and turned off his lights.

He looked around and saw nothing. It was only my imagination, he thought - I'm working too hard. What would a young girl be doing out on a night like this, especially in the pouring rain with only a night-gown on? He stopped for another moment, looked around again, shrugged it off as an overactive imagination, and continued on his way home.

He entered his house and after checking his phone messages, had a light lunch and a glass of wine. He decided to go to bed early. It was 9:40 and he had a long day ahead of him tomorrow. He sat in his favorite chair for a moment to rest his eyes. His mind drifted back to the little girl at the end of the road.

"I'm in the garden. Please come and talk to me," a soft voice pleaded.

What in the world is happening here, he thought. Reluctantly, he moved out of his chair, down the hall-way, and out into the garden. He looked around care-fully, but saw nothing. Just my imagination, nothing more, he thought. He listened another moment, heard nothing, and walked back into the house.

"Please don't walk away from me," the voice begged. "I'm here. Please talk to me."

As much as he did not want to turn, he did. There, in the middle of his garden, stood the little girl he had seen at the dead-end road. Her oval face had such a beautiful glow that it made him shiver.

"My God! Who are you?" he exclaimed.

The little girl did not speak for a moment, but continued to look at him as if she were looking beyond him. This can't be happening, he thought.

The young girl finally looked at him and spoke. "I have this feeling that I have known you all my life. I see you at a distance, but when I go to touch your hand, you move away from me. I have been trying to get you to listen to me, but when I reach out to shout at you, you seem not to hear me and you fade away."

Colin sat down on the patio chair, feeling he must be dreaming. Talking, as if to himself, he said, "That's it, I'm dreaming. This can't be happening to me ... it's crazy!" He was fixated on the girl and said, "Who are you? Why are you trying to contact me? Are you real or just an illusion?"

"I don't know," she answered.

At that moment, the image started to fade away and within a few seconds she was gone. After what seemed an eternity, Colin awoke, looked around, and found he was still sitting in his favorite chair in the living room. Thanks be to God! What a dream that was! Sometimes your mind plays all kinds of tricks on you.

That night Colin slept soundly, but with visions of the young girl in his mind.

When Colin awoke the following morning, the previous night seemed like a mysterious dream. He shook it off as overworking and decided to concentrate on today's work schedule. He had a meeting at 9:00 with two of his executives concerning the takeover of a small company in Port-aux-Basques, another meeting with a corporate lawyer about a corporate investment, and a new shopping mall in Carbonear. Then he had to make a visit to the Janeway Children's Hospital to present gifts to ill children. Colin didn't mind that too much, but it took up a lot of his time. Three hours meant a lot of time away from business, but he did commit to it so he had to see it through.

The day progressed quickly and at 2:30 he found himself an early Santa Claus for needy kids who could not be home for Christmas. He went from room to room with others, passing out gifts and was happy to see the smiles on the children's faces. It had been a long time since he had been in a hospital. So many sick kids, he thought, and they all seem so alone. Where are their parents?

As Colin continued on his course throughout the hospital with the group of volunteers, he passed by Room 505 and heard crying inside. Something compelled him to stop and go back as the others moved on down the hallway. He looked into the room and noticed a man and woman leaning over a bed, crying. He stood in the doorway for a moment and wondered what was happening. An urge overtook him and he made a few steps into the room.

"Excuse me," he said. "I was walking with my friends and heard you crying. Do you folks need anything?"

The man and woman sitting at the bedside turned and looked in his direction. "Who are you?" the man asked abruptly.

"I'm sorry. My name is Colin Pittman and I'm here with a group of friends for our annual trip to the Janeway to deliver Christmas gifts to the children."

"That's very commendable, Mr. Pittman, but I doubt gifts will ever help my daughter," the man stated.

He turned to look at his ailing child in the bed. Colin walked in and stared at the girl and nearly fainted. Lying in bed was the little girl he had spoken to in his garden! Mother of God, this can't be real! Colin felt his knees go weak, sweat poured off his brow, and his heart beat rapidly. He looked at the man and woman and in a barely audible voice, said, "The little girl - what is her name?"

The man looked at him, puzzled and confused. "She's our daughter, Melanie Harris," he replied.

"What happened to her?"

"This past summer, we were out in Terra Nova National Park on vacation when Melanie went swimming with her friends. She went under water for a few minutes before someone noticed she was in trouble." With trembling lips, he continued, "By the time we got to her, she had been under for three to four minutes. The paramedics tried to bring her around, but she was under too long. She has been this way ever since."

Colin looked at them both and said, "Please, Mr. and Mrs. Harris, do not think me crazy, but your daughter spoke to me last night in my garden. Call it a vision or whatever you wish, but she told me she had been reaching out to me for some time now, but every time she goes to touch me, I fade away. I know this sounds crazy, but would it be alright if I touch Melanie's hand?"

"This is crazy, indeed," Mr. Harris replied, "but we love our daughter and miss her very much. We are willing to try anything to reach her."

Colin approached the bed and softly whispered, "I'm here, Melanie. Now it's your turn to reach out and touch my hand."

Melanie moved slightly, opened her eyes, smiled, and put her hand in Colin's. She whispered, "I knew you would find me. Now I don't have to try and touch you anymore."

Mr. and Mrs. Harris were in shock. Colin bowed his head and tears flowed from his eyes. His thoughts immediately went to Rhonda and what a fool he had been not to have a beautiful child like Melanie. What a fool he had been to let his business and money get in the way of such beauty as this. This was what Christmas was all about, he thought. This was what it was all about!

"Call in a doctor to check her out," he told Mr. Harris. Melanie sat up in bed as her parents rushed to her side. Amid the hugging and kissing, Colin decided to leave the room. Mr. and Mrs. Harris looked at their daughter and rushed over to embrace Colin.

"I don't know what you did, Mr. Pittman, or how you did it, but my wife and I thank you from the bottom of our hearts. You have made this our happiest Christmas ever and we will never forget you for what you have done here today. How can we ever repay you?"

"Seeing Melanie awake is more than enough payment for me," Colin said.

Melanie looked at Colin as he was leaving and said, "I hope you will come and visit me at Christmas, Mr. Pittman. Don't forget to bring Rhonda with you too."

"I promise, Melanie."

Colin stayed until she was checked out by the doctors and, with another promise to see her again, he then left the hospital happier than he felt in many years. He got into his car and instead of attending his next meeting, picked up the phone and dialed his office number. Then it struck him ... how did Melanie know about Rhonda? He thought, *I guess in life there are things we do not understand and better off left alone,* but he was sure about one thing - he was going to change his way of living.

His cell phone had been dialing and then a voice at the other end said, "Good evening, Pittman's Investments. How may I help you?"

"Hi, Mary. This is Colin. Reschedule the rest of my appointments for today. I have something important to attend to that I should have done a long time ago."

"Certainly, Mr. Pittman. Is there anything else I can do for you?"

"Yes, phone the Janeway Hospital and find out how many children are admitted there. Then phone Toys R Us and make sure that every child in the hospital receives a gift. I don't care if it costs $200,000. And

Mary, make sure that Melanie Harris in Room 505 receives a special gift from me. Also, phone Flowers Unlimited and order a large arrangement for you and all the girls at the office. Finally, I'd like you to send two dozen of their finest red roses to my ex-wife, Rhonda."

After he hung up, he dialed Rhonda's number and got her voice mail. He said, "Rhonda, I know you will think me crazy, but I have had a life experience today that changed my way of thinking. Would you please spare me some time to sit down and tell you how stupid I've been to let you walk away? I love you. Please call me."

As he drove towards her house, he somehow knew that a vision of a little girl had forever changed his life.

- RJH

HAZARD MOUNTAIN
(By Lisa J. Ivany)

Nathan Cull peered around the end of the produce aisle of the Co-op grocery store, awaiting the victim of his latest prank. Within seconds, his best friend, Gerard Patey, came around the corner, whistling the tune of "Here Comes Santa Claus." Gerard pushed the trolley laden with fresh vegetables to one of the empty bins and proceeded to transfer celery stalks to the shelf. Suddenly, he screamed in fright and dropped the stalk he was holding to the floor.

From the end of the aisle, hysterical laughing erupted as Nathan and several co-workers had gathered to witness the joke. The look on Gerard's face as he unexpectedly saw the large plastic cockroach on the celery was priceless. However, he soon was laughing too as he realized the bug was not real and his friend had pulled another one over on him.

Nathan and Gerard had been working at the Co-op store in St. Anthony since they graduated from high school ten years before. Gerard, along with many other staff members, were often the recipients of Nathan's practical jokes, but the jokes were harmless and everyone had a good chuckle at them.

The two friends were very much alike in appearance with coal black hair, thick eyebrows, and rounded faces, looking more like teenagers than young men. Their aspirations in life were different in that Gerard was content to remain Produce Manager, while Nathan didn't want to limit himself to just being the store's main butcher. His passion was to someday be a well- known author and see his name plastered across a series of mystery books. He had started to write one in his spare time recently entitled, "Hazard Mountain."

"Hey Buddy, are we still heading for our week long trip to the slopes on Boxing Day?" Gerard asked Nathan.

"You bet we are," Nathan replied. "Kathy would kill me if I backed out now. She's been really looking forward to trying out her new skis that she somehow found out I bought her for Christmas."

"Yeah, I know what you mean. Nicole has had her suitcase packed for a week and she's been throwing hints for a new ski suit for Christmas. Needless to say, she will be quite pleased with Santa tomorrow morning when she unwraps her presents."

Three days later, the two couples traveled down the Northern Peninsula on their way to Marble Mountain in Corner Brook for a week's vacation. The journey itself was an enjoyable excursion with the sun shining from a cerulean sky and snow-capped fir trees stood majestically along the highway, looking like a typical Christmas card scene.

After checking into their two-bedroom cabin, the foursome wasted no time heading for the ski slopes. The bunny slope was tackled first to give Kathy a chance to adjust to her new skis. It only took a couple of trial runs for her to realize she was ready for the more challenging hills.

The girls whipped down the next slope as their husbands watched in admiration. Both girls were athletic with curves in all the right places. Kathy was of a shorter stature than Nicole and wore a purple ski suit trimmed with black and matching cap. Long strands of blonde hair cascaded down her back and billowed in the breeze as she descended the mountain. Her narrow face and thin nose were barely seen beneath thick snow goggles. Just behind Kathy, Nicole sliced down the slope, wearing her new green ski suit trimmed with hand-sewn embroidery. Her short auburn curls peeked out just beneath her gray angora cap next to her rosy red cheeks.

After the long day of driving and then repeated trips down the slopes, the group was exhausted by bedtime. Gerard and Nicole retired to their bedroom while Kathy went to bed alone, leaving Nathan to his laptop computer to write a few more pages of his story.

Nathan barely noticed the night speed by as he was so engrossed in his chapter about the mysteries of Hazard Mountain. He finished the chapter with a girl whose skis suddenly went airborne after hitting a log on the hill and she landed upside down in a tree with a fractured arm. Apparently, upon investigating the incident, the Mountain Patrol Officers could find no evidence of a log on the smooth run to have caused the accident. The only thing found at the scene was a red bow tied to the tree from which the girl had been suspended.

"Wake up, Nathan," Kathy's voice intruded.

"Huh, what?" he mumbled sleepily from his half-sitting, half-lying position at the kitchen table.

"Have you been out here all night?" she asked.

Rousing a little and coming to his senses, Nathan replied, "I guess so. I must have fallen asleep. What time is it?"

"It's time to hit the slopes, man," Gerard intervened, coming in through the front door with a load of firewood.

"I think I'll take a nap first and catch up with you

guys later," Nathan replied. "I didn't get much sleep last night."

By noon, Nathan pulled himself from the warmth and comfort of his cozy bed and made himself a cup of hot steaming coffee. The aroma itself stimulated his senses, rousing him to a state of alertness. After two thick slices of Kathy's homemade bread, toasted with peanut butter and marmalade, he felt ready to join his group outside. He was trying to remember what slope they said they were headed to, when the door burst open.

Kathy's concerned face was the first thing Nathan saw when he looked up from the table. Before he could question her, she was followed by Nicole, grimacing in pain, holding onto her right arm which was covered in a plaster cast. Gerard had his arm protectively about her shoulders.

"What happened?" Nathan exclaimed.

"Nicole had an accident on Spicer Hill this morning," Gerard replied.

"It was no accident!" Nicole shrieked. "I tell you, it was deliberate."

"What are you talking about?" Nathan questioned.

Nicole replied, "When I was halfway down Spicer Hill, out of nowhere a long tree log appeared in my path and there was no way for me to avoid it. My skis hooked into it and the next thing I knew, I was flying through the air and landed in a tree upside down. I was dangling there with my arm twisted behind me until the Mountain Rescue Team was able to get me down."

"That's when we brought her to the hospital and found out she had broken her arm," Gerard interrupted. "We don't really know what happened because the investigators checked it out and there was no log to be found. The only thing they found was a red bow tied to the tree Nicole landed in."

"Are you saying I'm making this up?" Nicole accused her husband.

"No, dear. Obviously something caused you to have the accident. However, you did take quite a smack to your head when you landed in the tree and maybe you thought you saw a log."

"I know what I saw and I don't appreciate your condescending tone."

Nicole shot him a look of contempt and strode into their bedroom, slamming the door behind her.

Gerard laughed uneasily and said to his friend, "I think the pain killers are affecting her brain."

Nathan replied, "This is so strange. The accident Nicole just described is exactly like the one I wrote about last night."

Later in the night, as the other three guests lay sleeping, once again Nathan sat in front of his computer screen, hatching up a new mystery for the next chapter of his manuscript. In this new scene, he had the husband of the first victim fall from a ski lift chair as it ascended the mountain. It was over quite a steep incline when the cable snapped, causing the character to land with quite an impact below. The force of the landing caused a severe sprain of his ankle and he had to be carried off the mountain with the aid of a stretcher from Mountain Patrol. They were puzzled about the accident as the cables were recently inspected and declared safe. When the accident site was checked later, it was obvious the cable had been cut, but the only thing found on the scene was a red bow tied to the cable.

Though he was on a roll, Nathan left his writing and went to bed in the wee hours of the morning. He didn't want to spend another night sleeping at the kitchen table. He realized he would need a good night's sleep to face the new hill that was opening tomorrow. He looked forward to racing down Suicide Run - Marble Mountain's most challenging slope yet.

"Good morning, sweetheart," Kathy said from the kitchen as Nathan emerged from their sleeping quarters. "There's a fresh pot of coffee on."

"Sounds good. Is Gerard up yet?"

"He's been up for a while. He couldn't wait any longer to get to Suicide Run so he said for you to join him over there when you're ready."

"It's only 7:00 a.m. How early does that guy get up?" Nathan laughed. "How's Nicole this morning?"

"She's still sleeping and I'm going to stay here with her for the day. You go and enjoy the slopes with Gerard."

"Are you sure?" Nathan asked. "I could stay here with you if you like."

"There's no need. You didn't get to ski at all yesterday so go and have some fun today. Nicole and I will be fine here."

At the ski lift next to Suicide Run, Nathan looked for Gerard, but he was nowhere to be seen. Nathan figured he'd find him at the top of the run and caught a ride on one of the ski lift seats. When he arrived at the top, he thought he spotted Gerard's teal jacket whiz by.

Rather than wait for Gerard to ascend the hill, Nathan thought he'd quickly ski down the run and meet up with his friend at the bottom. The weather had been cooperating since the start of their Christmas vacation and Nathan relished the feel of warm sunshine on his face and cool air flowing through his lungs as he sped down the mountain. Suicide Run was certainly a challenge with its twists, turns, and steep drops and was not for the inexperienced skier. Nathan felt a rush of excitement as he conquered each new obstacle and was elated upon reaching the bottom.

He heard a commotion before he noticed a group of people huddled in a circle. Not seeing his friend anywhere, he decided to have a look at what was happening over by the ski lift. When he arrived at the centre of the group, he saw the Mountain Rescue Squad tending to someone on a stretcher ... someone wearing a teal jacket. He raced over to the victim to find that it was Gerard.

"What happened?" he asked.

"I'm not sure," Gerard replied. "I was riding up in the ski lift when all-of-a-sudden, I was falling through the air and landed several hundred feet below. The medics here believe my ankle has a bad sprain, but no bones are broken. I guess I'm pretty lucky."

Nathan watched as his friend was carried away by the Rescue Squad, thinking how close he could have been to losing his best friend today. He noticed the ski lift had been shut down and the disabled chair was being scrutinized by the Chalet's staff members. His eyes scanned the seat and followed the course of the cable up to the top where he saw what looked like cut wires! Just below them a red bow danced in the breeze.

Nathan stood horror-struck, knowing that this was too much of a coincidence. The events he was writing about in his manuscript were becoming reality, but how could that be? What he was writing was a work of fiction totally out of his own imagination and yet it was happening in reality. There must be a logical explanation, he thought. The accidents themselves weren't inconceivable, but the red bows at the scenes, the same as in his book, could not be explained to his satisfaction and he had a deep sense of dread.

As Nathan walked the path to his cabin, he went over the events in his mind and finally came to peace with the realization that his imagination was going into overdrive. Of course there would be red bows displayed for the skiers in this festive season. It was

Christmas after all. They were probably attached to many trees on the ski runs to dress up the resort for the holidays. Perhaps if he had looked at all the ski lift chairs, he would have seen a red bow on every one of them.

"Hi, Nate," Kathy called from the doorway. "You're back pretty early. Did you find Gerard?"

"Yes, but he's had a little mishap on the slope."

"Oh no!" Nicole exclaimed, joining them on the bridge. "What kind of mishap?"

"It's nothing serious," Nathan explained. "He fell from the ski lift and sprained his ankle. The medics are taking care of him now and I'm sure he'll be back before dinner."

Nathan decided not to tell the girls about the similarities between his story and the reality of what was happening. He thought it would spook them and ruin the rest of their vacation. Besides, he thought it was all a coincidence and had explained it to himself logically anyway.

While Nicole rested and Kathy prepared dinner, Nathan hauled out his laptop and immersed himself into his manuscript once again. His perpetrator was becoming more aggressive now as he wired the ski resort's main chalet with explosives. The wires were hidden beneath the snow except for a few extending up behind the main stairs leading into the building. However, these would not be detected unless someone was actually looking for them.

A computer-printed note was sent to the main protagonist's wife, asking her to go to the main chalet to pick up a package. When she went inside the building, an explosion erupted and smoke billowed from the windows, however, the outside structure remained undisturbed. Even the culprit's signature red bow swung freely on the front door.

Nathan wasn't sure where to go with the story from here and put it aside for the moment as he heard the front door open. Gerard limped in with the help of crutches and was met by his wife who had scampered from the bedroom when she heard him come in. She wrapped her one good arm around his neck and hugged him tightly.

"Okay, missus," Gerard laughed. "You're choking me."

"I'm just glad to see you're alright," Nicole replied.

"We make a good pair of invalids, don't we?"

Nathan winked at Kathy and said, "Now, dear, you be careful near that hot stove or I'll be the only one around here who'll be able to cook dinner."

Kathy responded, "Heaven help us if that should happen. We've all tasted your cooking and barely lived to tell about it!"

Nathan retired at a more reasonable hour that night with his wife and had a full night's sleep. In the morning, he reached over to cuddle her, but she had already risen. He called out to her, but there was no response and the cabin seemed oddly quiet. He dressed and searched the rest of the cabin to find that Gerard and Nicole were also gone. Strange, he thought. They were barely able to get around with their injuries and yet they were gone out somewhere.

He then noticed a note lying on the table. Thinking it may be a message the rest of the gang had left for him, he picked it up. However, it was a typed note, asking Kathy to pick up a package at the main chalet. Fear seized Nathan's chest and he lost the ability to breathe. It was as though his book were coming to life and haunting him.

Nathan tore down the path to the main chalet, gasping as he pushed his legs beyond speed he had ever exerted before. There was a red bow on the front door that he hadn't noticed on his arrival three days earlier, but he rationalized that it could have blown off and been put back up later. He then checked behind the steps and to his horror, saw wires reaching up from beneath the snow. He raced through the chalet to the lounge where popping and cracking explosions ricocheted off the lodge's walls. This was accompanied by the sound of a throng of voices raised in unison, exclaiming "Surprise!" as he rushed in.

Nathan stood stock-still, surveying the room full of familiar faces, all smiling at him. The loud popping noises he heard were the corks from champagne bottles being shot off and the use of noise makers in the crowded room. He was amazed to see all his family, friends, and most of the staff from Co-op there to greet him.

Still stunned by what was happening and relieved that his wife was safe, he said, "What's going on?"

Gerard walked over to his friend without the aid of crutches and no longer exhibiting a limp and said, "Gotcha!"

"You mean this was all a prank?" Nathan asked in utter astonishment.

"Yes," everybody cheered in unison.

"Well, I say Bravo to you all," Nathan responded as he laughed and made a dramatic bow to the group. "But, how did you pull it off?"

Kathy said, "Each morning before you awoke, we read what you were writing and set up ways to transfer what was happening in your story to reality. Even getting them to stop the ski lift for a few minutes was easy when we told the owners what we were up to. In case you've forgotten, the new operator of the ski lift is Tony Williams who was the victim of many of your tricks when you worked together."

"I can't believe you all went through so much trouble to pull a fast one on me. I'm really impressed," he laughed. "However, now I feel really bad because I slashed the back tires of several of the cars out in the parking lot on my way in. When I thought Kathy was in danger, I went into a rage and started ripping tires. I'm really sorry." His look was one of such sincerity that most of the people in the room raced to the parking lot to check on their cars.

Nathan winked at Kathy and said, "They're so gullible." The sound of their squealing laughter could be heard by everyone in the parking lot as they looked at their perfectly intact tires. They realized they had been out-pranked once again by Nathan and laughter erupted in the parking lot to match the laughter inside.

Nathan walked out onto the front deck with Kathy in tow and said, "Gotcha ... and Merry Christmas!"

- LJI

If The Innkeeper Only Knew

If the innkeeper only knew
Who would be his guest that night
He would have had all his best
Prepared for the Messiah's arrival

If the innkeeper only knew
That he would be host to the world's Savior
Hallelujahs would be heard everywhere
Throughout Bethlehem

If the innkeeper only knew
That the angels would sing
The little drummer boy would play
Then rejoicing would fill his inn

If the innkeeper only knew
That the son of God
Would be born this night of nights
His best room would be at ready

But the innkeeper did not know
So the king of kings
Humbled Himself in a manger
And the world would never be the same

Robert J. Hunt

CHRISTMAS TRIVIA

Yule Log Legend

One story of this legend tells of the yule log being sprinkled with oil, salt, and mulled wine by the head of the household, who would then say a prayer over it. In other regions, a young girl in the home would light the log from leftover splinters of the previous year's log.

The yule log has been found to have its origin as far back as the days of the Vikings. The log was believed to bring good luck when burned in honour of the gods. This tradition was passed on to England in 1066 and spread to many other areas of the world.

The yule log tradition continues today, along with the belief of protection and good fortune.

Christmas Crackers

Christmas crackers were invented by an English confectioner by the name of Thomas Smith. The idea formed in Smith's mind when he visited Paris in 1844 and saw bonbons wrapped in tissue paper. He thought he'd add a motto and make the product more interesting by having the crackers open with a "bang!" Smith's new marketing idea was quite appealing to the public in 1846.

Smith originally called his novelty a "cosaque," which probably refers to the Cossacks from southern Russia. The Cossacks were famed horseback riders and were feared as soldiers.

The crackers contained a variety of inexpensive gifts and a verse. The Christmas crackers today often contain a paper hat, a joke or riddle, and a small toy, much the same as the original ones.

Festive Flavours

- Appetizers

- Brunch

- Vegetables

- Main Courses

- Desserts

NACHO DIP

2 - 8 oz pkgs cream cheese
¼ cup sour cream
¼ cup salad dressing or mayonnaise
1 tbsp taco seasoning
1-2 cups salsa
4 cups shredded lettuce
1 large tomato, seeded and diced
1½ cups shredded cheddar cheese
4 green onions, sliced

Beat cream cheese, sour cream, salad dressing, and taco seasoning with electric mixer until blended well. Spread onto bottom of large shallow dish.

Spread salsa over cream cheese mixture. Then layer with lettuce, tomatoes, cheddar cheese, and green onions. Use nacho chips or crackers to dip in.

HOT SWISS DIP

8 oz cream cheese
1½ cups shredded Swiss cheese
½ cup light salad dressing or mayo
 cup sliced almonds
2 tbsp chopped green onions

Preheat oven to 350.

Combine all ingredients together. Bake for 15 minutes; stir and then bake for another 15 minutes.

Use nacho chips or crackers for dipping. This is a rich dip so could be halved for only a few people.

PINE-NUTTY CHEESE BALL

12 oz cream cheese, softened
14 oz can crushed pineapple, well drained
1 tsp salt
¼ tsp onion powder
¾ cup pecans, chopped
2 tbsp red pepper, chopped
½ cup pecans, chopped (optional)

Combine cream cheese, pineapple, salt, and onion powder. Use electric mixer on low speed to combine. Stir in ¾ cup pecans and red pepper. Chill 2 hours and shape into a ball. Roll in ½ cup pecans if desired. Chill overnight. Serve with crackers.

SAUCY WIENERS

1 lb wieners, cut bite-size
½ cup ketchup
½ cup red currant jelly
1 tsp minced onion
1 tsp lemon juice

Combine ketchup, jelly, onion, and lemon juice in medium saucepan. Add wieners and bring to a boil. Cover and simmer slowly 30-45 minutes. Serve with toothpicks.

Makes 72.

JAPANESE CHICKEN SALAD

2 tbsp sesame seeds
½ cup slivered almonds
2 cups cubed cooked chicken
1 small head cabbage, grated
3 oz pkg instant chicken
noodles, crumbled
2 green onions, chopped

1 pkg noodle seasoning
½ cup salad oil
3 tbsp vinegar
1 tbsp sugar
1 tsp salt
½ tsp pepper

Put sesame seeds and almonds in a single layer in pan. Toast at 350 for 5 minutes or so, until golden. Remove from oven and set aside. Put chicken into large bowl; add cabbage, crumbled noodles, and onion.

In small bowl combine packet of seasoning, oil, vinegar, sugar, salt, and pepper. Stir together. Pour over chicken/cabbage mixture, then stir. Store in covered bowl overnight in fridge to marinate.

Just before serving sprinkle with sesame seeds and almonds. Toss lightly to distribute.

BROCCOLI SALAD

Salad:
1 bunch broccoli, washed and cut small
½ red onion, thinly sliced
6-8 slices bacon, fried and chopped
1 cup cheddar cheese (½ lb shredded)

Sauce:
¾ cup mayonnaise
2 tbsp wine vinegar
4 tbsp white sugar

Mix together sauce ingredients and then add salad ingredients. Mix together and refrigerate for three hours. Sesame seeds may be added if desired.

LAYERED SALAD

1 small head iceberg lettuce, shredded8 green onions, sliced
½ Romaine lettuce, shredded1 cup sour cream
1 cup celery, sliced1 cup salad dressing or mayonnaise
6 hard boiled eggs, sliced2 tbsp sugar
1¼ cup frozen peas, cooked1 cup shredded cheddar cheese
½ cup red pepper, chopped4 bacon slices, cooked and crumbled
8 slices bacon, cooked and crumbled

Combine both lettuces and line 9" x 13" pan. Next, layer as follows: Celery, eggs, peas, red pepper, first amount of bacon, and green onions.

Combine sour cream, salad dressing, and sugar. Pour over salad, being sure to spread completely to all edges of pan. Sprinkle with cheddar cheese and then second amount of bacon. Seal with plastic wrap and place in refrigerator for at least 24 hours before serving. Serves 10.

BAKED HOLIDAY OMELET

6 slices bacon, cooked and crumbled¼ cup red pepper, chopped
2 tbsp butter or margarine5 eggs
2 cups frozen hash browns½ cup milk

¼ tsp paprika tsp salt
¼ tsp celery salt tsp pepper
½ - 10 oz can mushroom pieces, drained¾ cup shredded cheddar cheese
  cup chopped onion   Preheat oven to 325

Fry hash browns in butter over medium-high heat in skillet until brown and crispy, about 7-8 minutes. Stir in paprika and celery salt and mix well.

Spray large pie plate or quiche dish with cooking spray and add hash brown mixture, spreading evenly. Cover with mushrooms, onions, and red pepper.

Whisk together eggs, milk, salt, and pepper. Pour over hash browns.
Bake 25 minutes, until set. Sprinkle with cheese and bacon pieces and return to oven until cheese is melted, about 2-3 minutes. Serves 6.

FRENCH ONION SOUP

4 medium Spanish onions
¼ cup butter or margarine
6 beef bouillon packets
6 cups water
½ tsp salt
2 cups croutons
¼ cup grated Parmesan cheese
1 cup shredded mozzarella cheese

Preheat oven to 450.

Cut onions into thin slices. Cut any long slices in half. In batches, sauté onions in butter until light golden brown.

In Dutch oven combine beef bouillon, water, and salt. Heat through and add onions. Cover and simmer ½ hour, until onions are completely cooked.

Ladle into oven-proof soup bowls and top with croutons, Parmesan cheese, and ending with mozzarella cheese. Bake until cheese is melted and browned. If preferred, this can be done under the broiler. Serves 4-6.

CHEESY CHOWDER

2 cups diced turnip
2 chicken bouillon packets or cubes
1 cup diced potato
2 cups water
1 cup diced onion
½ tsp salt
1½ cups diced carrot
¼ tsp pepper
¾ cup diced celery
2 cups shredded medium cheddar cheese

Place all ingredients, except potatoes and cheese, in large saucepan. Bring to a boil. Cover and simmer 15 minutes. Add potatoes and simmer another 15 minutes, until vegetables are tender. Do not drain. Stir in cheese until melted. Makes 5 cups.

BARBECUE CHICKEN WRAPS

6 small flour tortillas
2 boneless, skinless chicken breasts
¼ cup barbecue sauce
6 slices bacon, fried crisp and crumbled
1 medium tomato, chopped

¼ cup red onion, finely chopped
1 cup shredded cheddar cheese
Salad dressing or mayonnaise, to taste
Sour cream

Brush chicken with barbecue sauce and microwave on high 4-8 minutes, or until cooked through.
Chop in cubes.

Spread tortillas with salad dressing or mayo. Down one side of tortilla arrange chicken, bacon, tomato, onion, and cheese. Roll up fajita-style and secure with tooth-pick. Microwave on high until just heated through. Use sour cream for dipping.

TURKEY CHUNKERS

1 cup onion, chopped
1½ tbsp butter or margarine
2 cups cooked turkey, chopped
 cup salad dressing or mayonnaise
½ cup celery, finely chopped
1 tsp parsley
¼ tsp salt
Sprinkle pepper
 cup shredded cheddar cheese
8-10 hamburger buns   Preheat oven to 350

Sauté onions in butter until translucent and soft. Combine remaining ingredients, except hamburger buns, in bowl. Stir well to mix. Add onion and stir through gently.

Butter each half of hamburger buns and divide filling evenly among them. Wrap each bun in foil and bake for 15 minutes, until heated through. Serves 8.

TURNIP CASSEROLE

3 medium turnips
2 eggs, beaten
3 tbsp flour
1 tbsp baking powder
¾ tsp salt
 tsp pepper
Pinch nutmeg
2 tbsp butter or margarine
Pinch sugar

¼ cup bread crumbs
1 tsp melted butter or margarine   Preheat oven 375

Slice turnips and cook until soft. Add butter and mash. Add flour, baking powder, salt, pepper, nutmeg, butter, and sugar, mixing well by hand or with electric mixer.

Place in a greased 2 quart baking dish.

Combine bread crumbs and melted butter. Sprinkle over turnip mixture. Bake, uncovered, 25 minutes. Serves 6-8

VEGETABLE CHEESE LOAF

Layer 1:
2 eggs, fork-beaten
1 cup chopped broccoli, cooked
1 tbsp butter or margarine, softened
½ cup shredded cheddar cheese
¼ tsp onion powder
¼ tsp salt

Layer 2:
2 eggs, fork-beaten
1 cup cooked white rice
¼ cup red pepper, chopped fine
1 tbsp butter or margarine, softened
½ cup shredded mozzarella cheese
¼ tsp onion powder
¼ tsp salt

Layer 3:
2 eggs, fork-beaten
1 cup cooked carrot, mashed
1 tbsp butter or margarine, softened
½ cup shredded cheddar cheese
¼ tsp onion powder
¼ tsp salt   Preheat oven to 325.

Grease an 8 x 4 inch loaf pan. Combine first layer ingredients. Stir until butter is melted. Spread evenly in pan. Combine second layer ingredients. Stir until butter is melted. Spread over broccoli layer. Combine third layer ingredients. Stir until butter is melted. Spread over second layer.

Bake for about 1 hour.

FESTIVE VEGETABLES

1 tbsp cooking oil
1 cup carrots, sliced diagonally
1 cup celery, sliced diagonally
1 cup red pepper strips
1 medium onion, chopped coarsely
1 cup broccoli flowerets
1 cup fresh mushrooms, sliced

1 tsp garlic powder
½ tsp ground ginger
2 tbsp cornstarch
10 oz can chicken broth
1 tbsp soya sauce
Pinch sugar

Heat oil in skillet and add carrots, celery, and onion. Sauté until slightly softened. Add red pepper strips. Sauté 2 minutes. Add broccoli, mushrooms, garlic, and ginger. Sprinkle cornstarch over vegetables. Stir in broth, soya sauce, and sprinkle with sugar. Bring to a boil, stirring often. Reduce heat to low. Cover; simmer until vegetables are tender-crisp.   Serves 4

HASH BROWN CASSEROLE

1 pkg frozen hash browns
1 medium onion, diced
2 cups shredded cheddar cheese
2 - 10 oz cans cream of mushroom soup
1 cup sour cream
Corn flake crumbs

Preheat oven to 300.

Combine ingredients in large bowl, except for crumbs. Put mixture in a greased 9" x 13" baking dish. Sprinkle with crumbs. Bake 45 minutes.   Serves 8

BUBBLY FISH BAKE

1 lb frozen fresh cod fillets
10 oz can cream of mushroom soup
2 tsp chopped onion
3 tbsp water
1 tsp lemon juice
½ cup shredded cheddar cheese

Preheat oven to 400.

Cut frozen fillets into four portions. Place in a greased shallow baking dish.

Combine soup, onion, lemon juice, and water in bowl. Pour over fillets. Top with shredded cheese. Bake 20-25 minutes.
Serves 4.

GLAZED SALMON

4 tsp lime juice
3 tbsp liquid honey
2 tsp mustard
Salt and pepper, to taste
4 serving-size salmon fillets   Preheat oven to 350.

Combine juice, honey, and mustard in small bowl.

Sprinkle salt and pepper on both sides of salmon. Lay fillets in pan sprayed with cooking spray. Brush glaze over top of salmon.   Bake 25-30 minutes

BOXING DAY CASSEROLE

4 cups chopped cooked turkey or chicken
2 cups elbow macaroni
1 large onion, chopped
4-5 medium carrots, cut in short strips
1½ cups frozen peas
2 - 10 oz cans cream of mushroom soup
½ cup chicken broth
10 oz can mushroom pieces, undrained
½ tsp salt
 tsp pepper

Topping:

2 tbsp hard margarine or butter
½ cup bread crumbs
 cup shredded cheddar cheese

Preheat oven to 350.

Cook macaroni according to package directions; drain.

Place turkey and macaroni in 3 quart casserole. Add onion, carrot, celery, and peas.

Mix mushroom soup, chicken broth, undrained mushrooms, salt, and pepper in medium bowl. Pour over turkey and macaroni.

Melt margarine in saucepan and stir in bread crumbs and cheese. Sprinkle over top of casserole. Cover and bake for 1¼ hours, until carrot is tender. Remove cover and bake for 10 minutes, until topping is baked and lightly browned.   Serves 8

PINEAPPLE PORK CASSEROLE

1½ lb pork, cut into chunks¾ cup chopped celery
1 tbsp cooking oil¾ cup chopped carrot
1 medium onion, chopped2 tbsp soya sauce
2-4 tbsp brown sugar* cup ketchup
1 tsp salt cup water
Dash pepper19 oz can pineapple tidbits, reserving juice
2 tbsp vinegar10 oz can mushroom pieces, drained

Fry pork in oil until brown. Add remaining ingredients except for mushrooms and pineapple tidbits (reserved juice should be added). Bring to a boil and then simmer 1 hour. Add mushrooms and pineapple. Combine 1 tbsp cornstarch with 2 tbsp water. Add to pan. Simmer 5 minutes.

*Use 2 tbsp brown sugar if using sweetened pineapple or use 4 tbsp if using unsweetened.

CRANBERRY PORK CHOPS

6 pork loin chops1 cup whole cranberry sauce
Sprinkle seasoned salt3 green onions, sliced
Sprinkle pepper1 tsp brown sugar
1 tbsp margarine2 tsp cornstarch
1 cup apple juice½ tsp orange peel, finely shredded

Sprinkle pork chops with salt and pepper. Heat margarine in skillet and cook chops over medium-high heat to brown, turning once. Drain off fat.

Pour apple juice over chops and bring to a boil. Reduce heat. Simmer, covered, 40 minutes or until tender. Transfer pork chops to a platter, reserving ½ cup juice in skillet. Keep warm.

Combine cranberry sauce, green onions, brown, sugar, cornstarch, and orange peel. Stir into reserved liquid in skillet. Cook and stir over medium heat until thickened and bubbly. Cook for a further 2 minutes. Spoon sauce over chops. Serves 4-6.

CROWNED PORK & DRESSING

6-7 lb crown roast of pork
2 tsp salt
¼ tsp pepper
¼ tsp garlic powder
½ tsp Worcestershire sauce

Preheat oven to 325.
Combine salt, pepper, garlic powder, and Worcestershire sauce in small bowl. Rub into sides of meat. Place roast, with bone ends down, in roaster with a little water to cover bottom of pan. Roast for 2-2½ hours. Turn roast so that bones are on top. Put a sleeve of foil in centre of pork and add dressing. Cover with foil, poking 3-4 holes in foil with fork. If preferred, dressing may be cooked in dish separate from roast. Return roast to oven for 1½ hours.

Dressing:
6 cups bread crumbs
1 medium onion, chopped
1 medium apple, peeled and chopped
1 stalk celery, finely chopped
Pinch salt
Savory to taste

Combine all ingredients and blend well.

CHEESY BEEF AND MAC

1lb ground beef
½ cup chopped onion
10 oz can Italian tomato soup
1½ cups elbow macaroni
¾ cup water
 tsp pepper
1½ cups shredded cheddar cheese, divided

Preheat oven to 400.

Cook macaroni according to package directions. Drain. In skillet over medium heat, cook beef and onion until beef is brown and onions is tender, stirring to separate beef into small pieces. Drain. Stir in soup, water, pepper, cooked macaroni, and half the cheese.

Spoon mixture into 1½ quart casserole dish. Top with remaining cheese. Bake 25 minutes or until hot and bubbly.

CREAMY BEEF AND BROCCOLI

¾ lb beef sirloin steak
1 tbsp cooking oil
1 tsp garlic powder
1 medium onion, chopped coarsely
2 cups broccoli flowerets
10 oz can cream of broccoli soup
¼ cup water
1 tbsp soya sauce
Seasonings of your choice
6-8 cups broad egg noodles, cooked

Slice beef into thin strips. Cook half the beef strips with garlic powder and any seasonings you prefer, over medium-high heat in oil until beef is browned. Remove from heat and add second half of beef strips and cook until browned. Return all beef to skillet. Add broccoli and onion. Cook 5 minutes, stirring often.

Stir in soup, water, and soya sauce. Bring to a boil. Reduce heat to low. Cover; cook 5 minutes or until vegetables are tender. Serve over hot cooked egg noodles. Serves 4.

CHEDDAR BEEF PIE

1 lb lean ground beef
1 egg
1 small onion, chopped
1½ cups flaked corn cereal, crushed to ¾ cup crumbs
2-3 tbsp barbecue sauce
1 tsp salt
Pepper to taste
½ cup finely sliced celery
1½ cups shredded cheddar cheese
10 oz can mushroom pieces, drained
1 tbsp butter or margarine, melted
1 cup flaked corn cereal, crushed to ¼ cup crumbs

Preheat oven to 450.

Combine meat, egg, onion, ¾ crushed cereal, barbecue sauce, and seasonings; mix well. Press meat mixture around base and sides of 9 inch pie plate. Bake 15 minutes. Remove from oven and drain off excess fat. Reduce oven temperature to 350.

In a bowl combine celery, cheese, and mushroom pieces.

Toss lightly and spoon over meat mixture.

Combine melted butter with ¼ cup crushed cereal and sprinkle over cheese mixture. Return to oven and bake 10 minutes.

Serves 4-6

STEAK AND PEPPERS

1 large onion, cut in wedges4-6 green onions, chopped
1½ lb sirloin steak1 small red pepper, sliced
1 tbsp paprika1 small yellow pepper, sliced
1 tbsp cooking oil¼ cup soya sauce
1 tsp garlic powder cup water
1 tbsp sugar2 tbsp cornstarch
¼ tsp ginger2 large tomatoes, cut in wedges
10 can beef consommé

Pound steak to ¼" thickness and cut into strips. Sprinkle with paprika. Heat oil in skillet until hot and add beef strips and onion wedges. Fry until beef is browned. Add garlic powder. Sauté 1-2 minutes. Add consommé, sugar, and ginger. Cover and simmer 30 minutes.

Add green onions and peppers. Cover and cook 5 minutes.

In small bowl or cup combine cornstarch with water; add soya sauce. Stir into beef mixture and cook about 2 minutes, until thickened. Add tomatoes and stir through gently until heated, about 1 minute. Serves 4.

STUFFED ROLL

2 lb round or sirloin steak¼ cup bread crumbs
1-2 tbsp margarine¼ tsp salt
1 small onion, chopped tsp pepper
1 cup Parmesan cheese2 packets beef bouillon
½ cup fresh mushrooms, chopped2 cups boiling water

Preheat oven to 350.

Combine onion, Parmesan cheese, mushrooms, bread crumbs, salt, and pepper; set aside.

Pound steak thin. Spread cheese mixture over top and roll. Tie with string. Fry steak on all sides in margarine in skillet to brown. Transfer to small roaster that has been sprayed with cooking spray. Cover and bake 1½-2 hours, until tender. Serve in slices.

To make sauce, combine 2 tbsp flour with 4 tbsp water and stir into liquid in pan until it is blended. Bring to a boil until thickened. Serves 4-6.

SPAGHETTI BAKE

1½ lb ground beef
1½ tsp dried oregano, crushed
1 cup chopped onion
1 tsp salt
1 clove garlic, minced
1 tsp dried basil, crushed
28 oz can tomatoes, cut up
8 oz spaghetti, broken, cooked, drained
15 oz can tomato sauce

4 oz can mushroom pieces
1-2 cups shredded mozzarella cheese
2 tsp sugar
cup grated Parmesan cheese

In Dutch oven cook ground beef, chopped onion, and minced garlic until beef is browned and onion is tender; drain. Stir in undrained tomatoes, tomato sauce, mushroom pieces, sugar, oregano, salt, and basil. Bring meat mixture to boiling; boil gently, uncovered for 20-25 minutes, stirring sauce occasionally.

Remove meat sauce from heat; stir in drained spaghetti. Place half of the spaghetti-meat sauce in 9 x 13 inch baking dish; sprinkle with shredded mozzarella cheese. Top with remaining spaghetti-meat sauce; sprinkle with grated Parmesan cheese. Bake casserole at 375 for 30 minutes.

PIZZA CASSEROLE

1½ lb ground beef
1 medium onion, chopped
1 tbsp oil
10 oz can mushrooms, drained
1 pkg salami slices
3 cups macaroni
½ tsp garlic salt
19 oz can tomato sauce
1 pkg shredded mozzarella cheese
½ tsp basil
¼ tsp oregano

Preheat oven to 350.

Cook macaroni, drain and set aside. Fry onion and meat

in oil and drain. Add spices, mushrooms, and tomato sauce. Stir well. Add macaroni.

In 9" x 13" pan layer macaroni mixture, salami, and cheese.

Bake 20-30 minutes, until cheese is melted and lightly browned.

CHICKEN LASAGNA

3 cups fresh mushrooms
2 - 12 oz cans asparagus, drained
1 cup chopped onion
3 cups mozzarella cheese, divided in 3 parts
1 cup Parmesan cheese, divided in 3 parts
2 lb boneless chicken breasts, cubed
2 pkgs Hollandaise sauce, mixed according to package directions
1 tsp basil
1 tsp oregano
Lasagna noodles
Salt/pepper to taste

Preheat oven to 350.

Sauté mushrooms and onion in oil. Combine cubed chicken, basil, oregano, salt, and pepper. Cover and cook at 350 for about 1 hour to 1 hour 15 minutes, until cooked. Let cool.

In 9" x 13" pan assemble as follows:
Small layer of Hollandaise sauce

Layer of noodles
½ chicken mixture
½ mushroom/onion mixture
1 tin asparagus
1 part of both cheeses
Layer of noodles
½ of remaining Hollandaise sauce
Rest of chicken mixture
Rest of onion/mushroom mixture
1 tin asparagus
Second part of both cheeses
Layer of noodles
Rest of Hollandaise sauce
Rest of both cheeses

Cover with foil and bake for 35 minutes.

CHEWY SNOWBALLS
(From the story, *Maggie's Bread*)

2½ cups graham wafer crumbs
1 tin sweetened milk
1 tsp vanilla
4 squares melted unsweetened chocolate or 6-7 tbsp cocoa
Cherries

Mix above ingredients together and roll into balls. Roll in coconut. Flatten in middle of each ball with finger and add half a cherry.

Note: Put cherry in middle of each ball as you flatten each one. If you wait until all balls are flattened to add cherries, the mixture will be too hard for the cherries to stick.

FIVE STAR SQUARES

2 cups coconut
1 cup sweetened milk
2 cups graham wafer crumbs
1 cup butter or margarine

Melt butter in saucepan. Then add remaining ingredients. Bake at 350 for 9 minutes.

Icing:

½ cup butter
4 plain light chocolate bars with bubbles

Melt in microwave. Then stir and spread on top of mixture.

MAGGIE'S CHOCOLATE MARSHMALLOW ROLL

¼ cup hard margarine
1 cup icing sugar
1 cup mini coloured marshmallows
1 cup coconut
4 tbsp cocoa
1 egg

Cream margarine and icing sugar. Then add egg and cocoa and blend in.

Shape into a log. Then roll in coconut. Cut in slices or keep in refrigerator and then cut slices.

TOFFEE SQUARES
(From the story, *Maggie's Bread*)

½ cup flour
¾ cup crisp rice cereal
¼ tsp baking soda
Pinch salt
 cup melted butter
 cup brown sugar

14 oz can sweetened condensed milk
½ cup butter
½ cup brown sugar
½ cup chocolate chips
1¼ cups crisp rice cereal

Thoroughly combine first 6 ingredients. Press into a greased 8 inch square pan and bake at 350 for about 10 minutes or until just starting to brown.

In a heavy saucepan combine condensed milk, ½ cup butter, and ½ cup brown sugar. Over medium heat bring to a full boil and boil for 5 minutes, stirring occasionally. Remove from heat and pour over baked crust.

Melt chocolate chips and stir in cereal until well coated; spread (using two forks) on top of caramel. Chill several hours to set.

BOUNTY BARS

3¾ cups coconut
1 can sweetened condensed milk
6 plain chocolate bars with bubbles
1 tbsp oil

Combine coconut and sweet milk. Pat in bottom of square pan. Melt marshmallows in microwave 1 minute. Spread on top of coconut mixture.

Melt bars in oil in microwave and spread over marshmallow layer. Cool and cut into squares.

PECAN TARTS
(From the story, *Maggie's Bread*)

8 oz cream cheese, softened
1½ tsp vanilla
½ cup butter or margarine, softened
4 squares semi-sweet chocolate,
1½ cups flour each cut into 12 pieces
1 egg
1 cup pecans, finely chopped
¾ cup brown sugar, packed
2 squares semi-sweet chocolate,
1 tbsp melted butter or margarine melted
Preheat oven to 325.

Beat cream cheese and first amount of butter together. Stir in flour. Gather dough into a ball and add more flour if necessary. Divide into 48 balls. Place each into lightly greased mini tart pans. Press dough on bottom and sides of pans. Chill.

Whisk together egg, sugar, butter, and vanilla until well combined.

Place one piece of chopped chocolate and 1 tsp chopped pecans in the bottom of each pastry shell. Distribute filling evenly into each shell and sprinkle with remaining pecans.

Bake 20 minutes. Cool in pan 30 minutes. Drizzle melted chocolate on top. Chill. Makes 48

CHOCOLATE DROPS
(From the story, *Maggie's Bread*)

2¼ cups chocolate chips
1¾ cups butterscotch chips
¾ cup chopped peanuts
1½ cups crushed rippled potato chips

Melt chocolate and butterscotch chips in saucepan over low heat until melted, stirring often. Remove from heat and add nuts and chips. Stir to combine and spoon 1 tbsp into about 32 foil candy cups.

TOFFEE BAR DESSERT

1 pkg vanilla instant pudding
1 litre tub prepared whipped topping
 cup butterscotch sundae topping
6 chocolate toffee bars
1½ cups graham wafer crumbs
½ cup butter

Mix pudding according to package directions. Let stand 5 minutes or until slightly thickened. Mix together crumbs and melted butter and press into a square glass dish or springform pan. Spread butterscotch topping over the crumb mixture.

Fold whipped topping into pudding mixture along with 5 broken up bars. Put whipped topping mixture on top of butterscotch topping. Sprinkle on top with 6th bar, crumbled; then freeze. Serve frozen or thaw for 15-20 minutes before serving.

SEAWEED PIE

1 pkg chocolate cookie crumbs
½ cup margarine, melted
1 litre vanilla ice cream, softened
¼ cup sugar
1 large tub prepared whipped topping,
 2 chocolate & peanut flavoured bars softened
1 pkg pistachio pudding mix

Mix together melted margarine, crumbs, and sugar. Press into bottom of 9" x 13" pan.
Bake at 375 for 8 minutes. Cool before filling.

Mix whipped topping, dry pudding mix, and ice cream together and pour over base. Crumble bars and sprinkle on top. Dessert must be kept frozen.

NEAPOLITAN ICE CREAM CAKE

1 litre strawberry ice-cream, slightly softened
2 layer yellow cake mix
1 cups water
3 eggs
 cup vegetable or canola oil
2 oz unsweetened chocolate, melted and cooled slightly
 cup mini semi-sweet chocolate chips
1 small container liquid dessert topping, prepared
 cup chocolate fudge sauce, heated
Maraschino cherries, optional

Line 8" round cake pan with plastic wrap, leaving 2" overhang. Spread ice-cream evenly into pan; cover and freeze until firm.

Preheat oven to 350. Coat two 8" round cake pans with cooking spray. At low speed beat cake mix with water, eggs, and oil until combined. Increase speed to high and beat 2 minutes. Pour half the batter in one pan. Beat melted chocolate into remaining batter until combined. Stir in chips; pour into remaining pan. Bake 25 minutes, until toothpick inserted in centre comes out clean. Cool on racks 20 minutes. Remove from pans; cool completely on racks.

Place chocolate layer on serving plate. Remove ice-cream from pan; place on chocolate cake. Top with yellow cake layer. Ice cake with whipped topping and then drizzle with melted chocolate sauce. Freeze. Let stand at room temperature about 20 minutes before serving. Garnish with cherries if desired.

PISTACHIO TRIFLE

2 layer chocolate cake mix
1 pistachio pudding
2 envelopes whipped topping, prepared
4 chocolate wafer finger bars, crushed

Bake cake according to package directions; cool. Break into pieces.
Prepare pudding according to package directions; set aside. Mix pudding and whipped topping together. In large bowl, place a layer of cake cubes, then a layer of pudding mixture, and then a layer of crushed bars. Repeat layers, ending with bars.

CHOCOLATE TEMPTATION

2 layer chocolate cake mix
2 envelopes whipped topping
2 chocolate pudding mixes
2 tbsp coffee-flavoured liqueur
4 bars, of your choice, crumbled

Prepare whipped topping according to package directions; set aside. Prepare chocolate puddings according to package directions and add liqueur.

Cut cake into cubes and using a large deep bowl, put half the cake cubes in the bottom. Then layer half the pudding, half the whipped topping, and half the crumbled bars. Repeat layers, ending with bars on top. Serves 20.

PEACHY COOL DESSERT

½ cup butter or margarine
2 cups graham wafer crumbs
¼ cup brown sugar
28 oz can peaches, cut in pieces,
    drained - reserving juice
Reserved juice plus water to make
    2 cups liquid
¼ cup + 2 tbsp sugar
3 tbsp cornstarch
¼ cup cold water
8 oz cream cheese, softened
¾ cup sugar
2 cups whipping cream

Melt butter in saucepan. Stir in crumbs and sugar. Reserve ½ cup crumbs and press remaining crumbs into an ungreased 9" x 13" baking dish.

Combine peaches, juice combined with water, and first amount of sugar. Heat and stir until it boils and thickens. Add cornstarch combined with water. Stir to combine well. Cool.

Beat whipping cream until stiff. Beat cream cheese with second amount of sugar until light and fluffy. Add prepared whipped cream and combine well. Spread half cream cheese mixture over crust. Spoon peach mixture over top. Spoon remaining cream cheese mixture over peaches. Sprinkle with reserved crumbs. Chill. Serves 12-15.

Gift Basket Ideas

If you have trouble coming up with gift ideas for certain people on your Christmas list, perhaps a theme basket centered around their interests would be appropriate. Here are some ideas to get you started.

1. **Relaxation Basket (Fill Basket With):**

Aroma therapy candle   Foot Scrub
Relaxation cassette or CD   Bubble Bath
Mesh body scrubber   Bath Beads
Peppermint foot lotion   Pumice Stone
Bath pillow   Body Wash

2. **Cross Stitch Basket (Fill Basket With):**

A few skeins of floss   Line magnifier
Needles   Embroidery Hoop
Thread bobbins   Magnetic Board
Pattern book   Aida cloth
Floss storage container   Embroidery Scissors

3. **Gardening Basket (Fill Flower Pot With):**

Seed packets   Hand rake
Knee pads   Liquid fertilizer
Gardening gloves   Hand shovel
Plant stakes   Gardening book

4. **Movie Enthusiast's Basket (Fill Large Bowl With):**

Popcorn   DVD
Theater pass/video rental   Bag of candy
Large bottle of soda   Napkins

5. Office Worker's Basket (Fill Basket With):

Desk calendar	Notepads
Pens/pencils	Coffee mug
Recordable CD's	Mouse pad
Stapler	Desk clock
Business card holder	Paper clips

6. Pasta Lover's Basket (Fill Colander With):

Pasta cookbook	Jar of pasta sauce
Oregano, basil, thyme, etc.	Spaghetti tongs
Package of noodles	Olive oil
Parmesan cheese shaker	Oven mitts
Bottle of red wine	Checkered napkins
Pizza cutter	Cheese grater

7. Romantic Basket (Fill Basket With):

Candles/Snuffer	Massage oil
CD of romantic music	Romantic movie
Book of love poems	Bottle of wine
Bubble bath	Wine glasses
Lingerie	Chocolates

8. Writer's Basket (Fill Briefcase or Tote Bag With):

Pen	Journal
Lined stationery	Reference book(s)
Sticky notepads	Hole punch
Floppy discs or CDs	Letter opener
Pen grippers	Highlighters

Inexpensive Stocking Stuffers

1. Christmas tree ornament
2. Chocolate or candy
3. Crossword puzzle book
4. Blank cassette or CD
5. Flower or vegetable seeds
6. Stamp pad and stamper
7. Christmas brooch
8. Magnifying glass
9. Horoscope book
10. Disposable razors
11. Small stuffed toy
12. Novel or magazine
13. Hair accessories
14. Christmas mug
15. Jewelry cleaner
16. Refridgerator magnet
17. Sewing needles
18. Swizzle sticks
19. Address book
20. Deck of cards
21. Desk calander
22. Gift certificate
23. Coloring book
24. Small cookbook
25. Measuring tape
26. Night light
27. Tire gauge
28. Toothbrush
29. Mousepad
30. Bookmark
31. Small stapler
32. Diary
33. Keychain
34. Fishing lures
35. Snowglobes
36. Travel maps
37. Screwdriver
38. Flashlight
39. Calculator
40. Hand lotion
41. Harmonica
42. Bath beads
43. Vitamins
44. Nail clippers
45. Letter opener
46. Santa hat
47. Sun catcher
48. Candles
49. Kitchen timer
50. Wooden skewer

Ivany & Hunt

Christmas Card Register

Special Contacts	Year	20 __	20 __	20 __	20 __	20 __	20 __	20 __	20 __
Name:		Sent	Sent	Sent	Sent	Sent	Sent	Sent	Sent
Address:									
		Rec'd	Rec'd	Rec'd	Rec'd	Rec'd	Rec'd	Rec'd	Rec'd
Name:		Sent	Sent	Sent	Sent	Sent	Sent	Sent	Sent
Address:									
		Rec'd	Rec'd	Rec'd	Rec'd	Rec'd	Rec'd	Rec'd	Rec'd
Name:		Sent	Sent	Sent	Sent	Sent	Sent	Sent	Sent
Address:									
		Rec'd	Rec'd	Rec'd	Rec'd	Rec'd	Rec'd	Rec'd	Rec'd
Name:		Sent	Sent	Sent	Sent	Sent	Sent	Sent	Sent
Address:									
		Rec'd	Rec'd	Rec'd	Rec'd	Rec'd	Rec'd	Rec'd	Rec'd
Name:		Sent	Sent	Sent	Sent	Sent	Sent	Sent	Sent
Address:									
		Rec'd	Rec'd	Rec'd	Rec'd	Rec'd	Rec'd	Rec'd	Rec'd
Name:		Sent	Sent	Sent	Sent	Sent	Sent	Sent	Sent
Address:									
		Rec'd	Rec'd	Rec'd	Rec'd	Rec'd	Rec'd	Rec'd	Rec'd

Christmas Memories

Christmas Card Register

Special Contacts	Year	20__	20__	20__	20__	20__	20__	20__	20__
Name:		Sent	Sent	Sent	Sent	Sent	Sent	Sent	Sent
Address:									
		Rec'd	Rec'd	Rec'd	Rec'd	Rec'd	Rec'd	Rec'd	Rec'd
Name:		Sent	Sent	Sent	Sent	Sent	Sent	Sent	Sent
Address:									
		Rec'd	Rec'd	Rec'd	Rec'd	Rec'd	Rec'd	Rec'd	Rec'd
Name:		Sent	Sent	Sent	Sent	Sent	Sent	Sent	Sent
Address:									
		Rec'd	Rec'd	Rec'd	Rec'd	Rec'd	Rec'd	Rec'd	Rec'd
Name:		Sent	Sent	Sent	Sent	Sent	Sent	Sent	Sent
Address:									
		Rec'd	Rec'd	Rec'd	Rec'd	Rec'd	Rec'd	Rec'd	Rec'd
Name:		Sent	Sent	Sent	Sent	Sent	Sent	Sent	Sent
Address:									
		Rec'd	Rec'd	Rec'd	Rec'd	Rec'd	Rec'd	Rec'd	Rec'd
Name:		Sent	Sent	Sent	Sent	Sent	Sent	Sent	Sent
Address:									
		Rec'd	Rec'd	Rec'd	Rec'd	Rec'd	Rec'd	Rec'd	Rec'd

Ivany & Hunt

Christmas Card Register

Special Contacts	Year	20 __	20 __	20 __	20 __	20 __	20 __	20 __	20 __
Name:		Sent	Sent	Sent	Sent	Sent	Sent	Sent	Sent
Address:									
		Rec'd	Rec'd	Rec'd	Rec'd	Rec'd	Rec'd	Rec'd	Rec'd
Name:		Sent	Sent	Sent	Sent	Sent	Sent	Sent	Sent
Address:									
		Rec'd	Rec'd	Rec'd	Rec'd	Rec'd	Rec'd	Rec'd	Rec'd
Name:		Sent	Sent	Sent	Sent	Sent	Sent	Sent	Sent
Address:									
		Rec'd	Rec'd	Rec'd	Rec'd	Rec'd	Rec'd	Rec'd	Rec'd
Name:		Sent	Sent	Sent	Sent	Sent	Sent	Sent	Sent
Address:									
		Rec'd	Rec'd	Rec'd	Rec'd	Rec'd	Rec'd	Rec'd	Rec'd
Name:		Sent	Sent	Sent	Sent	Sent	Sent	Sent	Sent
Address:									
		Rec'd	Rec'd	Rec'd	Rec'd	Rec'd	Rec'd	Rec'd	Rec'd
Name:		Sent	Sent	Sent	Sent	Sent	Sent	Sent	Sent
Address:									
		Rec'd	Rec'd	Rec'd	Rec'd	Rec'd	Rec'd	Rec'd	Rec'd

Christmas Card Register

Special Contacts / Year	20 __	20 __	20 __	20 __	20 __	20 __	20 __	20 __
Name:	Sent	Sent	Sent	Sent	Sent	Sent	Sent	Sent
Address:								
	Rec'd	Rec'd	Rec'd	Rec'd	Rec'd	Rec'd	Rec'd	Rec'd
Name:	Sent	Sent	Sent	Sent	Sent	Sent	Sent	Sent
Address:								
	Rec'd	Rec'd	Rec'd	Rec'd	Rec'd	Rec'd	Rec'd	Rec'd
Name:	Sent	Sent	Sent	Sent	Sent	Sent	Sent	Sent
Address:								
	Rec'd	Rec'd	Rec'd	Rec'd	Rec'd	Rec'd	Rec'd	Rec'd
Name:	Sent	Sent	Sent	Sent	Sent	Sent	Sent	Sent
Address:								
	Rec'd	Rec'd	Rec'd	Rec'd	Rec'd	Rec'd	Rec'd	Rec'd
Name:	Sent	Sent	Sent	Sent	Sent	Sent	Sent	Sent
Address:								
	Rec'd	Rec'd	Rec'd	Rec'd	Rec'd	Rec'd	Rec'd	Rec'd
Name:	Sent	Sent	Sent	Sent	Sent	Sent	Sent	Sent
Address:								
	Rec'd	Rec'd	Rec'd	Rec'd	Rec'd	Rec'd	Rec'd	Rec'd

Christmas Card Register

Year Special Contacts	20 __	20 __	20 __	20 __	20 __	20 __	20 __	20 __
Name:	Sent	Sent	Sent	Sent	Sent	Sent	Sent	Sent
Address:								
	Rec'd	Rec'd	Rec'd	Rec'd	Rec'd	Rec'd	Rec'd	Rec'd
Name:	Sent	Sent	Sent	Sent	Sent	Sent	Sent	Sent
Address:								
	Rec'd	Rec'd	Rec'd	Rec'd	Rec'd	Rec'd	Rec'd	Rec'd
Name:	Sent	Sent	Sent	Sent	Sent	Sent	Sent	Sent
Address:								
	Rec'd	Rec'd	Rec'd	Rec'd	Rec'd	Rec'd	Rec'd	Rec'd
Name:	Sent	Sent	Sent	Sent	Sent	Sent	Sent	Sent
Address:								
	Rec'd	Rec'd	Rec'd	Rec'd	Rec'd	Rec'd	Rec'd	Rec'd
Name:	Sent	Sent	Sent	Sent	Sent	Sent	Sent	Sent
Address:								
	Rec'd	Rec'd	Rec'd	Rec'd	Rec'd	Rec'd	Rec'd	Rec'd
Name:	Sent	Sent	Sent	Sent	Sent	Sent	Sent	Sent
Address:								
	Rec'd	Rec'd	Rec'd	Rec'd	Rec'd	Rec'd	Rec'd	Rec'd

Christmas Memories

Christmas Card Register

Special Contacts	Year	20 ___	20 ___	20 ___	20 ___	20 ___	20 ___	20 ___	20 ___
Name:		Sent	Sent	Sent	Sent	Sent	Sent	Sent	Sent
Address:									
		Rec'd	Rec'd	Rec'd	Rec'd	Rec'd	Rec'd	Rec'd	Rec'd
Name:		Sent	Sent	Sent	Sent	Sent	Sent	Sent	Sent
Address:									
		Rec'd	Rec'd	Rec'd	Rec'd	Rec'd	Rec'd	Rec'd	Rec'd
Name:		Sent	Sent	Sent	Sent	Sent	Sent	Sent	Sent
Address:									
		Rec'd	Rec'd	Rec'd	Rec'd	Rec'd	Rec'd	Rec'd	Rec'd
Name:		Sent	Sent	Sent	Sent	Sent	Sent	Sent	Sent
Address:									
		Rec'd	Rec'd	Rec'd	Rec'd	Rec'd	Rec'd	Rec'd	Rec'd
Name:		Sent	Sent	Sent	Sent	Sent	Sent	Sent	Sent
Address:									
		Rec'd	Rec'd	Rec'd	Rec'd	Rec'd	Rec'd	Rec'd	Rec'd
Name:		Sent	Sent	Sent	Sent	Sent	Sent	Sent	Sent
Address:									
		Rec'd	Rec'd	Rec'd	Rec'd	Rec'd	Rec'd	Rec'd	Rec'd